THE
ARTISAN
KITCHEN

THE ARTISAN KITCHEN

JAMES STRAWBRIDGE

THE SCIENCE, PRACTICE, & POSSIBILITIES

Photographic Art Direction James Strawbridge
Photography John Hersey
Illustrations James Strawbridge

Project Editor Holly Kyte
Project Art Editor Miranda Harvey
Senior Editor Alastair Laing
Senior Designers Karen Constanti, Saffron Stocker
Managing Editor Dawn Henderson
Managing Art Editor Marianne Markham
Senior Production Editor Tony Phipps
Senior Producer Luca Bazzoli
Jacket Designer Saffron Stocker
Jacket Co-ordinator Lucy Philpott
Art Director Maxine Pedliham
Publishing Director Mary-Clare Jerram

First published in Great Britain in 2020 by
Dorling Kindersley Limited
DK, One Embassy Gardens, 8 Viaduct Gardens,
London SW11 7BW

A CIP catalogue record for this book
is available from the British Library.
ISBN: 978-0-2413-9977-4

Printed and bound in China

For the curious
www.dk.com

For Indiana, Pippin, and Arrietty
I hope that this book helps you look after our "pets" and inspires you to keep cooking xxx

Contents

Foreword

For too long we've been separated from the ingredients that go into our cooking, but now, we're rediscovering that connection and realizing how accessible artisan food is.

Many of the ingredients we use in our everyday cooking aren't raw but the culmination of someone else's artisan journey. Cheese, bread, preserves, sausages – they've all been made and developed by someone else. As soon as you start to realize this, it empowers you to go on a culinary adventure of your own and make artisan ingredients from raw produce.

By understanding the science behind the practice, developing an awareness of the processes, and following the practical steps, you will find that, as a result, something everyday can suddenly be wrapped in pride. With a little time, patience, and knowledge, we can achieve anything in the kitchen. And the health benefits, the fun of collaborating with others, and the overwhelming feeling of satisfaction when we make our own artisan food is well worth the effort.

In this book, I've captured a host of artisan skills that are deeply rooted in our cooking heritage. Over thousands of years, cooks have learned how raw natural substances can be transformed by mixing them together or applying heat, smoke, or air, triggering all sorts of fascinating chemical reactions. Understanding these reactions is hugely beneficial to the artisan cook, so first I've provided a basic summary of the science behind each process. I like to view cooking as a creative experience, too, however, so for the recipes themselves, I've updated the classics and then offered possibilities for you to experiment with. You will learn how to churn your own butter, bake your own sourdough, make your own jam, and smoke your own garlic. Start by mastering the basics, then practise the classics, and finally let your flair and creativity come out to play.

Time and patience are two of the most valuable commodities in an artisan kitchen, and this applies to so many aspects of the craft. Sourdough ferments slowly. Charcuterie can take weeks to air-dry. Many of the projects in this book take longer to cook than a quick meal in the evening after work. Nonetheless, they can still be fitted in around a busy lifestyle at the weekends or simply checked on every day or two if they're an ongoing project – and all this extra time is used well, as it intensifies flavours and allows the preserving methods to do their job.

In a way, I think these traditional crafts are part of the remedy for the fast pace of modern living. By slowing down, we can afford ourselves time to appreciate the ingredients we're using and the people around us. Foraging outside to reconnect with the wild larder, meeting other artisan producers to exchange culinary secrets, and mentally rejuvenating all help you return to the kitchen refreshed, ready to focus on your food. This is probably the most valuable lesson I've learned in my cooking career so far. When people have one foot in the kitchen and the other in the office, they have a tendency to drop one of their spinning plates. Mindfulness is very of the moment, but in a kitchen it's essential.

The other vital ingredient in an artisan kitchen is a team of friends, family, and other keen cooks to keep you inspired. The foodie community has gone through so much change in recent years, with the growth of digital platforms and social media sending cooks into a spin. When once we talked and shared family recipes, now we tune in to Instagram posts from around the world depicting the perfect meal,

with styled food photography and deliberate props. If you want a taste of the real artisan kitchen, find your local foodie network. Visit farmers' markets. Talk to other keen cooks, artisans, and older generations to learn from them about producing food in less of a rush and with more attention to detail. Everyone has to start somewhere, so my advice is to engage with your family first, then your friends, and then open the doors of your kitchen wide to other local artisans who are experts in their field.

Much of my knowledge comes from being self-taught, but I've been able to progress thanks, in part, to artisan producers who have openly shared with me their top tips, warnings, and success stories. Their passion always motivates me to have a go myself, so for *The Artisan Kitchen* I invited fellow chefs, artisans, and friends to cook with me. I had the pleasure of learning how to pat butter properly in a one-on-one lesson with 86-year-old Barbara; I got new fermenting ideas from Irish cook Rose; I made traditional Gouda

cheese with Dutch farmer Giel; I got stuck in to charcuterie with Marc; I got sourdough tips from baker Tom; I discovered new smoking techniques with Ty; I went full salt geek with Philip; I bottle-conditioned cider with Barrie; Andy demonstrated some serious chef skills with his bresaola slicing; Tia fuelled my passion for plant-based cooking; I shared farmhouse dairy stories with Francis, and had tons of outdoor cooking fun with Ed. Now I have the privilege of passing all that on to you.

I want this to be an open book – collaboration has taught me so much, and in a way, I'm just forwarding on this collective knowledge, because no one person owns our culinary heritage. It's yours and mine and belongs to our children. Yes, I've added a few creative twists of my own, but this book is for all of us. The journey towards the artisan kitchen is a great learning experience, and I hope this book inspires you on yours.

James Strawbridge

Kitchen Basics

It may sound predictable for a chef to start with advice from the classical French school of cookery, but for me, when discussing a kitchen, it all begins with the phrase *mise en place*. This means having everything in its right place before you start – ingredients peeled, measured, sliced, and grated; tools and equipment clean and laid out in an organized fashion. Since I started working in kitchens over 20 years ago, I've learned from the bottom up that organization and preparation make for the best cooking environment and the tastiest food.

The basics for a functional and pleasant kitchen are the following: a clean and well-organized space to work in; a selection of tools that have been sharpened and well maintained so that they are efficient; and local, seasonal, top-quality ingredients. To assemble the recipes in this book quickly, effortlessly, and to best effect, I cannot encourage you enough to prepare your kitchen and get everything you need together in one place, ready for the challenge ahead.

Hygiene

Impeccable hygiene is essential for successful artisan projects, so always remember the adage of "clean as you go". This is particularly important for these traditional projects, because you're dealing with raw produce and bacteria, and using no chemical preservatives, so if things aren't clean, the food could become dangerous to eat.

CLEANING

Equipment tends to be put through its paces with the effects of salt cures, smoke residue, vinegar, and heat, but if you look after your kit, it will look after you. Cleaning down thoroughly after each project and habitually scrubbing your oven between cooking sessions will stand you in good stead. It is also worth oiling or seasoning cast-iron tools and scouring pans so that they don't rust in between use.

STERILIZING

Sterilizing your tools and containers, such as preserving jars and lids, before you begin any project is good practice. Wash items in hot soapy water, then boil in clean water for 5–10 minutes. Spread out the items on a baking tray to allow good air circulation and then dry them in a preheated oven at 140°C (285°F) for 15 minutes. This will kill all yeasts, fungi, and bacteria. Fill preserving jars while still hot from sterilizing if possible.

LABELLING

If, like me, you catch the bug for rediscovering artisan kitchen crafts, you will quickly find that you have numerous projects on the go at the same time. To keep all your produce safe and tasty when multi-tasking, ensure that you label things clearly with what they are, the date you made them, and the use-by date. Also, set reminders for when to revisit ferments, charcuterie, and slow-cooking recipes. This attention to detail should also apply to storage. Stay organized and rotate your fridges and larder, bringing older items to the front to use first and putting new preserves at the back, so that you don't lose something valuable in your own enthusiastic productivity.

Tools and Equipment

The artisan kitchen does require some specialist equipment, which can improve the quality of what you produce and determine how easily you can make certain recipes at home. Most of what you need can be stored in the kitchen and used in your normal cooking, making it easier to justify the expense. If you are enthusiastic about artisan kitchen crafts, then you will find that your toolkit will quickly grow. My advice would be to store your equipment so that it's readily to hand. For example, I keep my kit in a large flight case, toolbox, and small shelving unit. Being organized means you can really enjoy the flexibility of being able to set up a field kitchen, with everything together for easy access.

If you invest in good-quality kit, it is likely to last longer. I tend to buy equipment that would be just as at home in a professional kitchen as a domestic one, in the knowledge that it will last a lifetime and provide a great deal of pleasure downstream. Most kitchen tools are easily available online, and if in doubt, ask your local butcher, cheesemaker, charcuterie expert, or baker for advice.

MACHINERY

One of the key benefits of artisan crafts is that they are relatively low impact, with very little modern machinery required. The traditional crafts can be mastered with old-fashioned hand tools, but if you are keen on making your own sausages and salamis, or pressing your own cheese, then think about buying yourself specialist equipment, such as a mincer and sausage-filling machine or a cheese press. There are hand-powered versions available for mincers, mills, and presses.

If you are enthusiastic about artisan kitchen crafts, then you will find that your toolkit will quickly grow.

Figure a.

KNIVES

Knives are to chefs what feet are to dancing. They are our tools, friends, and foes. You can often learn a lot about a chef from how they look after their knives. Get yourself a knife roll, magnetic strip, or knife block and store your knives safely. They are always looking for a way to dull their keen edges or chip their tips, but the answer is simple: don't keep knives in a drawer or leave them to be bashed about on the draining board; wash them up carefully, then dry them and return to the block, and sharpen them regularly.

Knife Sharpening
This is somehow seen as a dark art, but sharpening knives is easy. You have a few options, all with their own merits.

STEEL
I use a steel several times a day. I often sharpen a knife in between kitchen services to keep myself on point. The advantages of using a steel are that they are portable, discreet and easy to use in a small space, and efficient for a fine edge. Never get your steel wet, and if you can afford it, get yourself a diamond sharpening steel. The abrasive surface produces an optimum edge and they can have up

to two million diamond grains applied to the surface. They will wear out and become smooth over time, though, so may need replacing.

To sharpen using a steel, hold your knife in your chopping hand and the steel in your non-dominant hand (**fig. a**). Hold the steel facing upwards and draw the knife downwards from the heel to the tip of the knife at a 15-degree angle. Maintaining control each time, repeat on alternate sides, and wipe your knife on a cloth before cooking. Keep your body posture tight, working close to your body to avoid injuring anyone else in the kitchen. Some cooks love to show off with a steel, swishing their knife through the air away from themselves, but don't be intimidated by their bravado; instead, see a steel for what it is: a highly functional tool for all cooks.

WHETSTONE

If you want to sharpen all your knives in one session or work on a knife that has really lost its edge, get yourself a whetstone and dedicate 30 minutes to doing a few in one go. I use a whetstone every few weeks. Soak your whetstone before use in a bowl of water (without any detergent), then with a cloth or towel nearby to clean the blade, start by carefully using the coarse side of your stone at a 15–20-degree angle (**fig. b**). Always make sure that the angle you sharpen at is the same on both sides of your blade. If you grind at different angles, you can actually end up dulling the edge. Carefully apply pressure to the blade and slide it down your stone. Repeat this a few times and then do the same number of strokes on the other side. Once you feel that the blade is sharp, turn over your stone and use the finer surface to finish. If your blade is sharp, you should see very little or no light bouncing off the edge. Any nicks or dents will catch the light.

ELECTRIC KNIFE SHARPENER

A large number of chefs use electric knife sharpeners (**fig. c**), because they're fast and efficient. They are also a little noisy. They can be a useful tool if you have lots of knives to sharpen, though, as they certainly save plenty of time.

Figure b.

Figure c.

A Guide to Knives

There is a knife for every job, but like many cooks, despite having a large collection of knives, I still have a few favourites that I use 90 per cent of the time. They are my most treasured tools and I believe that investing in a good set of blades for different jobs provides endless satisfaction and a much easier cooking experience. My top tips would be to get the following specialist knives in your roll:

CHEF'S KNIFE

Possessing an all-round chef's knife is a must. You will find that it becomes key to your kitchen practice.

BONING KNIFE

To cut out bones from a pork belly or to debone a chicken. This knife is easy to move around meat and can transform what you can achieve with DIY butchery. It is sharp, narrow, and flexible – perfect for crevices and carving out as much meat as possible.

MEAT SLICER

This isn't as necessary as the others for everyday use, but to be an authentic pit master or home butcher, it certainly makes you look the part! A slicer is perfect for brisket or salmon; it is a long, thin, slightly flexible blade that cuts long, even strokes perfectly. Often it will have a scalloped Granton edge to reduce sticking when cutting.

SCIMITAR

A versatile scimitar is excellent for general butchery, raw meat prep, and slicing. It is heavier than most knives and curved at the tip, so you can rock it back and forth for easy chopping.

MEAT CLEAVER

Ideal for vegetable prep but also for cutting through bone without causing splintering. A butcher's cleaver should be strong and relatively heavy.

If you want to explore specialist blades in more detail, visit a knife shop to ask for advice.

CONTAINERS

Given the range of methods in this book, from curing to fermenting, baking to brining, it is worth investing in a range of containers or bins that you can use for these processes. Avoid containers and equipment that could corrode or rust. I try to use glass rather than plastic, despite the fact that it's heavier and more expensive, because I know it'll last longer and is infinitely recyclable. Purchasing a selection of different-sized containers, ranging from one small enough for curing bacon to one large enough for brining a ham or brisket, is a good move. Also, instead of recycling, keep all your glass jars – sterilize and reuse them for chutneys, pickles, jams, and ferments.

STRING

When I visit my local butcher for meat, I tend to ask for some butcher's string at the same time, because it is food safe, easy to tie, and durable. Hanging meat and fish or tying up salami is best done with butcher's string. It is also very useful for hanging herbs and chillies to dry or for suspending jellies and cheese curds to drain.

Knife essentials
A selection of chef's knives, a steel, and a whetstone.

Figure d.

Figure e.

AIR CIRCULATION EQUIPMENT

Muslin or cheesecloth allow air to circulate around products while still protecting their surfaces against contamination from pests and insects. If you are air-drying produce outside, you may want to consider building a drying box that can protect the food and still allow ventilation. For this, I'd recommend hanging the box under a porch so that it's relatively protected from the weather.

HOOKS

I always make sure that I have an array of butcher's hooks in different shapes and sizes. They can be used in the fridge to optimize space and are very useful in smokers or for air-drying food in a well-ventilated room.

BRINOMETER

This is a useful gadget to measure the exact salinity of brine solutions. A brinometer can measure the percentage of salt in a solution at room temperature. They are easily available to buy online and are often sold by cheesemaking shops.

PREPARATION TOOLS

Other key tools that are useful for food preparation and may be worth investing in are:
- **For seafood:** fish slice, filleting knife, tweezers, shucking knife **(fig. d)**.
- **For veg prep:** fine grater, scissors, tomato knife, Japanese mandoline, spiralizer **(fig. e)**.
- **For meat:** meat probe, syringe, poultry shears **(fig. f)**.

Figure f.

Ingredients

My journey with food started with ingredients. Growing my own fruit and vegetables, or rearing chickens, pigs, and goats, has always encouraged me to use all of the ingredient and attempt to do it justice. Sourcing local and seasonal ingredients is my passion, and then preserving them to be enjoyed over the coming days, weeks, and months is intoxicating. To find the best ingredients, my advice is to get out to your local markets and forage for seasonal treats on coastal paths or in the hedgerows. Visit farms to buy direct, and support the artisan food movement by joining their network. Weave your way into the foodie scene and you will be amazed at the sense of community and the free exchange of knowledge. When you buy ingredients, think about where they come from and how fresh they are. I am a massive fan of native and zero-waste menus and will always try to buy local, seasonal, and organic food. I also hate to throw anything away, so I try to be creative with all parts of my food, from root to peel. The methods in this book should help you to avoid food waste and provide creative ideas to reduce what goes in the compost bin.

SEASONALITY

Seasonal food is precious due to its limited availability. The season for ripe strawberries is so precious because in a moment it's gone. Treasure seasonal produce by committing to cooking and preserving it, but also embrace a feeling of festive celebration. If blackberries are only going to be on the bramble for a few weeks, then that's the time to go mad and make jam or ferment, pickle, and dehydrate them with real energy in the kitchen. I don't allow a doom-and-gloom outlook on food miles or the rise of processed alternatives in my kitchen. Instead, I focus on the good things – the ripe fruit and lush greens; the simple things we can appreciate – and when I'm in the kitchen I throw myself into working with what's fresh, seasonal, and local to me. To make a real change, choose something that you love to eat and don't want to give up, then start making it yourself from quality ingredients that are in season. You'll never look back.

SUSTAINABILITY

I love supporting local farmers' markets and buying directly from farms. When I can't get organic ingredients, I think it matters to buy seasonally and locally. There are now lots of online retailers who sell fruit and veg boxes, organic meats, and MSC (Marine Stewardship Council) certified seafood. Other sources of sustainable food that I particularly enjoy are the wild game season and going out on fishing trips. For me, sustainability is key to the artisan kitchen, and while I don't want to sound preachy, I think it is one of the motivating factors behind preserving good-quality food.

Treasure seasonal produce by committing to cooking and preserving it, but also embrace a feeling of festive celebration.

FORAGING

Living in Cornwall near the coast means that, fortunately, I have access to moorland, woods, and coastal foraging. I'd argue that wherever you live there will be pockets of delicious free food to forage. I harvest berries, fruit, seaweed, nuts, and leaves from the coastal paths and farmland near my home and it never ceases to amaze me how the flavours can be so pure and intense. I use foraged ingredients to subsidize my ferments, add seasoning to cures, or enliven bread with added colour and texture. Edible flowers are fantastic dried and preserved in salts for a floral note, rosehips make a syrup rich in vitamin C, while dried seaweed is great to cook with – as crisps or as a seasoning with umami depth. Try to build a foraging walk into your weekly kitchen routine to strengthen your grasp on seasonal food and inspire new flavour combinations. It will also help you to build perspective and remember that we are all part of a large, complex food system. The outdoor kitchen is where all of us get our food from, and I like to connect with the wild side as well as the more clinical kitchen processes.

PRESERVES

Project 01
SOUR-FERMENTED PICKLES

Tangy condiments fizzing with gut-friendly bacteria.

SKILL LEVEL Medium: fermentation needs careful observing and tasting.

TIMINGS 30 minutes prep; 2 hours for osmosis; 1–3 weeks fermentation time.

Plate of pickles
Typical sour pickles include sauerkraut, kimchi, and carrots.

THE SCIENCE

Lacto-fermentation

Unlike pickles that rely on vinegar for preservation, sour pickles extend shelf life and gain their tangy flavours through lacto-fermentation. In a natural process, beneficial bacteria munch away at the glucose in vegetables and fruit, drawing on stored energy by converting the molecules into lactic acid. This partial breakdown of plant sugars, and their acidic by-product, creates a host of palatable flavours, which have a near-miraculous ability to enhance the taste of other foods.

LACTO-BACTERIA

The heroes of lacto-fermentation are some real tough cookies of the bacterial world, a gang of friendly microbes able to survive in brutally acidic and saline conditions and who thrive in an anaerobic environment. Strains of these bacteria are naturally present on the surfaces of most vegetables and fruit, and in the right environment are only too pleased to start multiplying. Handily, the same conditions that lacto-bacteria enjoy and create – acid, salty, oxygen-free – inhibit the "bad" bacteria and moulds that would otherwise cause produce to rot. What's more, as the lacto-bacteria digest and ferment the raw ingredients, they impart a pleasing sourness to the pickle. Also worth mentioning is that eating lacto-fermented pickles helps to boost gut flora, which research increasingly shows is vital for general health.

SALT OSMOSIS

Osmosis is another natural process key to sour pickling: the propensity of water to penetrate a permeable barrier, in order to balance out the concentration of chemicals dissolved either side of the barrier. By rubbing salt over vegetables and fruit, water is drawn out and salt drawn in, until the amount of salt dissolved is equal inside and out. The liquid produced is often enough, once ingredients are packed into a jar, to create the anaerobic environment beloved of lacto-bacteria – so don't throw it away!

Anaerobic controls
Prevent air from getting at the ingredients to keep any bad bacteria at bay.

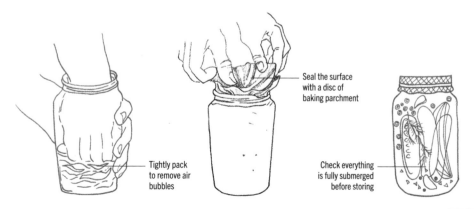

Tightly pack to remove air bubbles

Seal the surface with a disc of baking parchment

Check everything is fully submerged before storing

THE PRACTICE

Pink Pickle

Beetroot balances the subtle metallic tang of a ferment with a sweet earthiness, which works well with crispy cavolo nero and fresh raspberries. For a tart dressing, use the vibrant pink pickle juice to finish off the dish.

MAKES

1-litre (1¾-pint) jar

INGREDIENTS

½ red cabbage, finely sliced
3 beetroot, peeled and grated
2 red onions, finely sliced
fine sea salt

EQUIPMENT

1-litre (1¾-pint) preserving or
    fermentation jar, sterilized
masher (optional)
pestle or rolling pin
muslin or cheesecloth (optional)

Method

01   Prepare your vegetables **(fig. a)**, then weigh them and
calculate 2 per cent of the total weight to find the
amount of salt you need (total weight in grams ÷ 100
× 2 = amount of salt in grams). In a large bowl, evenly
cover all the pink veg with the sea salt **(fig. b)**.

02   Using a masher or your hands, break up the veg **(fig. c)**
to allow the salt to penetrate the maximum surface
area, then leave covered for a few hours or overnight.

03   Transfer the salted vegetables, with any juice, to a
preserving jar and use a pestle or rolling pin to push
the veg down, removing any air pockets.

04   Leave to ferment in a warm place (18–22°C/65–72°F)
for 10–14 days, leaving the jar unsealed for the initial
fermentation period so that the gases can escape. I
often cover the jar with muslin or cheesecloth and
secure with an elastic band, or if you are using a
fermentation jar with a valve, the valve should be open.

05   Seal and label the jar, then store in a slightly cooler
place (18–20°C/65–68°F), and check every week for the
first month to release any further gas from this slower,
secondary fermentation. Store for 12–24 months.

EXPERT TIPS

A warm environment will help
speed up the fermentation process
and your veg will be more likely to
be fully fermented within the
specified 10–14 days. However, if
you ferment at a slightly lower
temperature the flavour of your
pickle will be deeper.

———

Blitz all the ingredients in a food
processor before fermenting them
to create a paste to add to hummus
for a tangy flavour.

———

The fermented pickle juice makes a
fantastic salad dressing. Try the
sour pink pickle with crispy kale,
raspberries, and orange zest.

Figure a.

Figure b.

Figure c.

THE PRACTICE

Rainbow Chard Kimchi

Kimchi is a spicy fermented dish from Korea traditionally made with cabbage. Here, chard supplies the same textural mix of soft leaves and crunchy ribs and stalks, while the fermenting process foregrounds the earthy, almost smoky beetroot flavours of this root vegetable relative. Try experimenting with other leafy greens, such as kale, pak choi, and collards.

Figure a.

Figure b.

Figure c.

MAKES

1-litre (1¾-pint) jar

INGREDIENTS

large bunch of rainbow chard
    (around 500g/1lb), leaves
    roughly shredded and stalks
    chopped into large chunks
bunch of dill, finely chopped
2 fat garlic cloves, sliced
5cm (2in) knob of ginger, peeled
    and finely chopped
1 or 2 red bird's eye chillies,
    finely chopped
fine sea salt

EQUIPMENT

1-litre (1¾-pint) preserving or
    fermentation jar, sterilized
pestle or rolling pin (optional)

Method

01 Prepare enough chard to fill the preserving jar almost
    to the top, tightly packed in. Test the fit and weigh the
    chard. Prepare the dill, garlic, ginger, and chilli but keep
    separate (**fig. a**); weigh these as well, then set aside.
    Measure out 2–3 per cent of the total weight in salt.

02 Place the chard in a large bowl and sprinkle over the
    salt. Massage the salt into the chard, until it begins
    to release beads of water and starts to soften (**fig. b**).
    Leave for a couple of hours to let osmosis take effect.

03 Place the salted chard and any juices into the jar,
    scattering over the herbs and spices with each handful.
    Pack in the vegetables tightly, pressing them down
    as you go and eliminating air pockets between layers.
    Use a pestle or the end of a rolling pin to tamp down
    the ingredients (**fig. c**).

04 Top up the jar with water, if needed, so that the
    vegetables are submerged. Cut a disc of baking
    parchment large enough to cover the contents of the
    jar, with some excess. Place the disc over the vegetables,
    pressing it down and into the edges to ensure the
    surface is completely covered.

05 Seal the jar and date and label the contents. Leave to
    ferment at room temperature, out of direct sunlight,
    for 1–2 weeks. Taste regularly after 1 week, until the
    preferred degree of sourness is reached, then transfer
    to the fridge, where it will keep for several months.

EXPERT TIPS

Spread the salt over the greatest
surface area to increase osmosis:
massage thoroughly and get it
right into any crevices.

———

The parchment keeps ingredients
submerged to maintain an
anaerobic environment. A plastic
bag filled with air is an effective
alternative, or you can buy jars
with built-in airlocks.

———

Look out for small bubbles
of carbon dioxide, a sign that
fermentation is in full swing. If the
process is slow to get going, try
moving the jar to a warmer spot.

THE PRACTICE

Golden Kraut

Sauerkraut has its roots in ancient Mongolia, but nowadays it has a distinctive Germanic or Eastern European vibe. The method can be adapted for a whole host of vegetables from around the world; red cabbage, fennel, celeriac, and carrot kraut are all worth trying. For a bit of extra flavour add juniper berries, ginger, caraway seeds, or dill.

MAKES

2 x 500ml (16fl oz) jars

INGREDIENTS

1 whole cabbage, such as savoy,
    white, hispi, Chinese, kale,
    or other brassicas
1 tbsp freshly grated turmeric root
    (optional)
fine sea salt

EQUIPMENT

mandoline (optional)
pestle or rolling pin
2 x 500ml (16fl oz) preserving
    or fermentation jars, sterilized
fermentation weights (optional)

Method

01 Finely slice your cabbage (a mandoline is a time-saver here) and combine in a bowl with the grated turmeric root, if using **(fig. a)**, then calculate 2 per cent of the total weight to find the amount of salt you need (total weight in grams ÷ 100 × 2 = amount of salt in grams). Cover the veg evenly with the salt, then massage the cabbage with your hands **(fig. b)** to break down the cellulose and encourage osmosis.

02 Leave overnight and then use a pestle or rolling pin to ram the salted cabbage into the jars, ensuring that you squeeze out the air pockets and completely submerge the cabbage in its own brine to provide an anaerobic environment. If necessary, press the cabbage beneath the surface with fermentation weights **(fig. c)**.

03 If using fermentation jars, open the valve, or leave the preserving jar lids loose enough to allow the gases to escape while the kraut ferments.

04 Leave to ferment at room temperature (18–22°C/ 65–72°F – warmer if you want a fast ferment, cooler if you want a slower, more full-bodied ferment) for 10–14 days. Then seal, label, and leave until you want to serve. Once opened, keep refrigerated and use within 1 week.

EXPERT TIPS

As an alternative to fermentation weights, ensure that the top layer of cabbage is covered with a small disc of baking parchment that you push down underneath the brine.

———

If you want to create an even more colourful version, add in some peeled, thinly sliced, or grated beetroot, which will stain the whole ferment purple (or yellow if you use golden beetroot). They will also provide an earthy grounding note to the tang of kraut. Aim for 25 per cent beetroot.

Figure a.

Figure b.

Figure c.

THE POSSIBILITIES

Play with Form

Lacto-fermentation can be unpredictable, but with experience you will learn to manipulate this living process to produce endlessly fascinating new flavours.

PURÉES AND POWDERS

Fermented vegetables are versatile so experiment with forms.

- Carrots, beetroot, and potatoes are all excellent fermented whole with 2 per cent salt **(fig. a)** but can also be blitzed into smooth fermented purées that make tangy vegan dips: try with ribbons of raw vegetables and some radicchio for contrasting bitterness.
- Blitz vegetables in a food processor before fermenting for a lower-effort ferment that's a fast-track to flavour. Use a rough paste mixed well with 2–5 per cent salt to ferment garlic or chilli peppers in bulk. The fermented purée can then be used in kimchi or curries.
- Dehydrate your ferments by placing on baking trays in a very low-temperature oven (50°C/120°F) or using a dehydrator (see pp.58–61), until the texture is dry enough to crumble or blitz in a spice blender. Use these complex powders to season with umami depth. They look colourful and taste fantastic as a seasoning for root crisps or as a garnish for fresh vegetables **(fig. b)**. The downside is that the beneficial bacteria will be killed off, so they don't possess the same health benefits as raw fermented food.

Figure a.

Figure b.

Figure c.

Figure d.

IF IT GROWS, FERMENT IT

Look beyond cabbages to evolve your
conception of sour pickling.

- Pickle fruit: fermenting develops sharpness
  while still preserving the dominant
  sweetness. Fermented foraged blackberries
  or haw berries make a lovely base in an
  autumnal ketchup (see recipe, right) or to
  garnish game dishes. Fermented green
  strawberries are great with fish. Even green
  tomatoes, apples, or rhubarb can be
  fermented to preserve the harvest and
  enhance their natural depth of flavour.
- Combine adventurously: pair vegetables
  with contrasting textures and flavour profiles,
  or shake up veg pickles with fruit accents.
  I also add edible flowers to some fermenting
  batches for subtle floral notes.
- Go naked and ferment vegetables simply
  on their own with nothing other than salt.
  Sliced pumpkin makes a fantastic ferment in
  its simplest state, deseeded but with its skin
  on for a bit of texture **(fig. c)**. Serve this
  torched on one side for a contrast between
  the sweet tang and woody char. It's really
  good with duck, but also experiment with
  it for a pumpkin pie that is off the charts.

Try ... Fermented haw berry ketchup Soften
1 finely diced shallot in a drizzle of oil, add 200g
(7oz) sugar, 350ml (12fl oz) red wine vinegar and
250g (9oz) haw berries **(fig. d)** or blackberries. Add
a pinch of salt, paprika, and chilli flakes, then cook
slowly over a low heat for 30–45 minutes until the
vinegar has reduced and the ketchup has thickened.
Pass through a sieve to remove small kernels and
stems, then blitz until smooth – particularly good
with wild boar sausages and venison burgers.

*The longer a pickle is left to ferment
the more sour it becomes. While you
may enjoy a mouth-puckering blast
of sourness, too much can overwhelm
more subtle flavours.*

Feeding your body beneficial bacteria that improve your gut flora while exciting your taste buds is a practice rooted in the past but deeply forward-thinking. Fermentation is the ultimate preserving method, but it's also a way to explore everyday ingredients anew – by unlocking flavour and making food that's good for you, too.

Project 02
VINEGAR PICKLES
The fastest way to add acidic notes to a dish.

SKILL LEVEL Easy.

TIMINGS 20 minutes
prep; 1–2 hours to
pickle before serving.

Beyond gherkins
Sliced onions, cauliflower
florets, even girolle
mushrooms all make
great vinegar pickles.

THE SCIENCE

Preserving with Vinegar

Vinegar pickles are a simple and speedy way to preserve fruit and vegetables while locking in freshness and elevating flavour. Produce is immersed in a hot solution of vinegar, water, spices, and salt (and sometimes sugar) and the acetic acid in the vinegar, aided by the heat, prevents decay – although for a longer shelf life, brining beforehand is essential. An acidic bite stimulates saliva, so pickles are literally mouth-wateringly good.

AN ACIDIC ENVIRONMENT

Vinegars generally have an acidity level of 5 per cent and a pH level of less than 4.6, which inhibits the growth of most microorganisms and prevents botulism spores from germinating. The downside of such a highly acidic environment is that it causes food to lose its nutritional value over time, so vinegar pickles are best enjoyed within 4 weeks. Unlike fermented pickles, vinegar pickles are "cooked" to further kill off bacteria, which can affect the texture of your produce. For a fresh refrigerated pickle with crunch, the temperature should be hot but still comfortable to touch. If you immerse veg in an extremely hot solution, you can preserve them for longer but the cellulose structure will degrade more quickly and the pickles can become soft within 2–4 hours.

THE ROLE OF BRINING

For pickles you intend to keep unrefrigerated for longer than 4 weeks, brining or dry-salting the veg first for 12 hours is necessary (see below). This stage enhances flavour, as the salt penetrates the veg through osmosis before being discarded (see p.19). It also draws out water, adding crispness and preventing the moisture from leeching out later, which would dilute the pickling liquor's acidity and reduce the vinegar's effectiveness at killing harmful microbes. As a guide, use 250g (9 oz) of salt to 2.5 litres (4¼ pints) of water for a strong brine.

Salting for longer life
Through osmosis, salt draws water out of vegetables, which prolongs life by removing moisture that would otherwise dilute the vinegar's acidity.

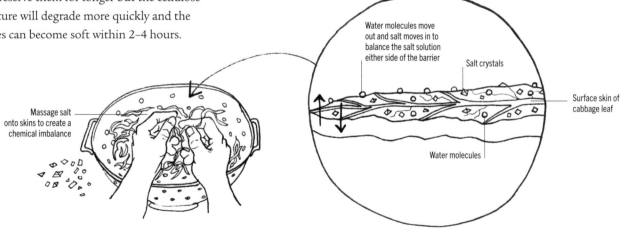

Massage salt onto skins to create a chemical imbalance

Water molecules move out and salt moves in to balance the salt solution either side of the barrier

Salt crystals

Surface skin of cabbage leaf

Water molecules

THE PRACTICE

Piccalilli

Piccalilli is an iconic British pickle. Its heritage can be traced to colonial India, where the vibrant tradition of pickling vegetables with rich, colourful spices was quickly taken up. The process involves a bit of planning – dry-salting the vegetables the day before – but it's worth it. Turmeric and mustard add plenty of depth, and the resulting pickle is superb paired with cold meats and cheese.

Figure a.

Figure b.

Figure c.

MAKES

4 x 500ml (16fl oz) jars

INGREDIENTS

450g (1lb) cauliflower florets, chopped into teaspoon-sized pieces

450g (1lb) whole Silverskin pickled onions

450g (1lb) cucumber, deseeded, and chopped into 1cm (½in) pieces

450g (1lb) French beans, trimmed

100g (3½oz) fine sea salt

750ml (1¼ pints) white malt vinegar

1 tbsp mustard powder

1 tbsp ground ginger

1 tbsp ground turmeric or 2 tbsp freshly grated turmeric root

1 tbsp yellow mustard seeds

175g (6oz) golden caster sugar

2 tbsp cornflour

EQUIPMENT

heavy-based, stainless-steel preserving pan

4 x 500ml (16fl oz) preserving jars, sterilized

Method

01   First, prepare the vegetables for dry-salting **(fig. a)**, then put them in a non-metallic bowl. Sprinkle the salt over the top, toss together to coat evenly, cover, and leave in a cool place for 12 hours.

02   The next day, put the vinegar into a large preserving pan along with all the spices and bring to the boil.

03   Drain the dry-salted vegetables and rinse well under running water to remove the salt.

04   Add the vegetables to the simmering vinegar **(fig. b)** and cook over a low heat for 25 minutes, then add the sugar and continue to simmer for a further 2–5 minutes.

05   Mix the cornflour with a little water and blend into the hot vinegar solution. Bring back to the boil and cook for a further minute. The piccalilli mixture should be glossy and thick.

06   Remove from the heat and leave to cool for 15 minutes. Spoon the mixture into jars, then seal **(fig. c)** and label. Store in a cool, dark place for 3–4 weeks to allow the flavours to mature and mellow before eating.

EXPERT TIPS

If using your own produce, gather fruit and vegetables intended for preservation when ripe, in the morning, and ideally in dry weather. This harvest will have the fullest flavour and keep for the longest.

———

A stainless-steel pan is necessary for vinegar pickling, as copper, iron, and brass pans can spoil when exposed to high acidity.

———

Ensure that the salt you use is free of anti-caking agents. Conventional table salts contain additives that may turn your clear pickling liquor cloudy. Use a fine sea salt so that it dissolves quickly.

THE POSSIBILITIES

Sharp and Sweet

Addictive, sweet-sour vinegar pickles can lift any dish
– they're quick, easy, and versatile, and add bursts of
colour and taste sensations like no other kitchen craft.

CREATIVE GARNISHES

Paint splashes of colour across your plate and
create adventurous flavour pairings with
pickled garnishes.

- Red onions are maestros of alchemy **(fig. a)**.
  In a white wine or cider vinegar they will
  transform from earthy red to bright pink –
  a staple garnish for tacos and salads.
- Match spices to your pickles and celebrate the
  colourful nature of food. For pink pickled
  onions use a garlic clove, chilli flakes,
  peppercorns, and fennel seeds for warmth.
- Use colourful spices to dye muted veg with
  bold pigments. Try charcoal baby turnips, or
  for a luminous cauliflower pickle infuse the
  vinegar with turmeric, yellow mustard seed,
  ginger, and cumin **(fig. b)**.
- Pair seasonal flowers, herbs, and aromatics
  with your pickles. With something earthy like
  pickled mushrooms or girolles, use rosemary
  or thyme, juniper, and clove.

TASTE OF THE SEA

Throw cooked shellfish into a pickle solution
for a pop of zingy sharpness. You can also mix
filtered seawater with the vinegar to bring that
seashore tang to life.

- Pickled mussels with pan-roasted fish and
  a creamy butter sauce will cut through the
  richness of the dish.

Figure a.

Figure b.

Figure c.

• Pickled cockles served simply with lemon juice, celery salt, and Tabasco are timeless.
• Pickled sardines with paprika, pickled carrot, and fennel as an escabeche can be sublime.

Try ... Pickled mackerel Cure 2 mackerel fillets in a salt cure of 50g (1¾oz) sugar and 50g (1¾oz) sea salt for 1 hour, then wash clean under a cold tap and pat dry. Slice the fish into even, bite-sized pieces and immerse in a hot sweet vinegar pickle made with 75ml (2½fl oz) white wine vinegar, 2 tablespoons of water and 30g (1oz) sugar, and flavoured with 1 tablespoon of seaweed flakes. Leave in the hot vinegar solution to cool for 20–30 minutes, then serve in a clean oyster shell with horseradish cream, some cucumber pickles **(fig. c)**, and dill.

GET FRUITY

Cut through the sweetness of fruit by pickling in a sharp vinegar solution.
• Hedgerow fruit and autumnal berries are excellent served with duck or venison.
• Halved figs in a red wine vinegar pickle are superb with cured meats and blue cheese.
• Vary your pickles across the season and experiment with walnuts or stone fruit.

Try ... Rhubarb and ginger Thinly slice 2 stems of rhubarb. Add 1 tablespoon of sliced root ginger and cover with a 1:1 vinegar and water solution, with some sugar added to taste and a pinch of salt, for a fresh pink pickle to accompany mackerel, tofu, or spicy stir-fries. Keep refrigerated and eat within 2 weeks.

> "
>
> *A good vinegar pickle will punctuate a plate with lively notes, keeping your taste buds engaged like a jazz musician following a rhythm that alternates between ingredients and leaves you wanting more.*
>
> "

Project 03
CHUTNEY

A spicy relish of preserved fruit or veg with an intense vinegar tang.

SKILL LEVEL Easy: balancing the acidity and sweetness takes practice, but as a preserving method this is achievable for beginners.

TIMINGS 30 minutes prep; 2–3 hours cooking.

Harvest chutney
Chutney is a recipe in which all the taste senses can be tickled in one jar.

Vinegar Reduction

Derived from eastern India, chutney preserves fruit and vegetables by cooking them in vinegar and sugar, often with added spices for aromatic flavour, until most of the liquid has reduced and the texture has become thick and jam-like. The sugar, acidity, and long cooking time work together to inhibit bad bacteria, providing an effective way to preserve a harvest glut, as well as an instant dollop of rich, tangy-mellow flavour.

ACIDITY

The primary preserving agent in a chutney is the acetic acid in the vinegar (see Vinegar Pickles, p.31), as well as the natural acid in the fruit. To prevent the growth of pathogenic bacteria, moulds, and yeasts, chutney needs a high acidity level because these organisms, which would otherwise cause the ingredients to rot, cannot survive in an acidic environment. A pH level below 4.6 is ideal (I use litmus paper to test pH levels) – this should ensure your chutney is safe for long-term consumption.

MOISTURE

When making a preserved chutney, the core principle is to cook the mixture for long enough to allow most of the liquid to evaporate; apply the wooden spoon test to check when your chutney has reached the correct consistency (see right). Reducing the moisture level in this way further kills off any

unwanted microorganisms, which cannot survive without water. The sugar in chutney is also vital to this process, because in a concentrated sugar solution, bacteria lose water as a result of osmosis, causing them to denature. Many commercial manufacturers add unhealthy amounts of sugar (i.e. more than is needed for the purpose of preservation), which results in extremely sweet chutney, so by making your own you can control the sugar levels. If you want to make a quick chutney to enjoy young, within a week, you can use less sugar and slightly less vinegar and cook for a much shorter time. If you are aiming for a long shelf-life, however, all the basic scientific principles of preservation should be adhered to for a safe and consistent end product.

Draw a wooden spoon across the bottom of the pan – it should leave a clear trail

Water vapour

Bubbles

Moisture reduction Evaporation helps achieve the right consistency for chutney and aids preservation.

THE PRACTICE

Harvest Chutney

This chutney has it all: sweetness, acidity, earthy spices, and that slow-cooked umami depth. It's my grandpa's recipe, which I've tweaked over the years, and as with all good chutneys, it's about cooking the produce for long enough to transform its texture to a jam-like consistency. If you can't get hold of green tomatoes, slightly underripe or ordinary tomatoes also work brilliantly.

MAKES

2 x 500ml (16fl oz) jars

INGREDIENTS

olive oil, for frying
1 onion, finely diced
2 garlic cloves, finely chopped
1 tsp ground allspice
1 tsp ground ginger
1 tsp paprika
1 tsp chilli flakes
1 tsp coriander seeds
½ tsp ground cinnamon
½ tsp ground nutmeg
1.5kg (3lb 3oz) green tomatoes,
    roughly chopped
2 Bramley apples, peeled, cored,
    and sliced
100g (3½oz) sultanas
2 litres (3½ pints) cider vinegar
1kg (2¼lb) caster sugar
1 tsp salt, or to taste

EQUIPMENT

heavy-based, stainless-steel
    preserving pan
2 x 500ml (16fl oz) preserving jars

Method

01 Add a little olive oil followed by the onion, garlic, and spices to a large preserving pan and fry over a low heat until softened **(fig. a)**. Before the onions brown, add in the tomatoes, apples, and sultanas.

02 Simmer over a low heat, stirring every 5 minutes or so **(fig. b)**, for 45 minutes, until the apples and tomatoes are nicely cooked. They should have a soft texture while still retaining some shape in the pan (I don't like my chutney completely broken down, as I like to see what I'm eating).

03 Add the vinegar and simmer for a further 1–2 hours, remembering to stir occasionally at first and then more attentively as the liquid reduces to avoid burning the bottom of the pan. Add a dash more vinegar if the liquid is reducing too quickly.

04 Once the mixture has thickened, add the sugar and stir until dissolved, then season to taste with the salt. Cook for a further 15–20 minutes over a medium-high heat until the mixture is thick enough for you to draw your spoon across the bottom of the pan and leave a clear trail behind (see p.37).

05 Spoon the chutney into jars and fill them to the top to minimize the presence of oxygen **(fig. c)** and aid preservation. Seal and label the jars, and keep for 6–12 months. Allow to mature for at least 2 weeks before enjoying. Once opened, store in the fridge.

EXPERT TIPS

The ratio for chutney is around 6:2:1, so, for example, 3kg (6½lb) raw prepped ingredients to 1 litre (1¾ pints) vinegar to 500g (1lb 2oz) sugar. Using this as your starting point, you can devise your own chutney recipes, experimenting with different ingredients, vinegars, and sugars.

_____

Remember to stir the mixture at the bottom of the pan, not just the top. Due to the sugars, chutney can burn easily, which will taint the preserve with a strong charred flavour. Keep it moving and, if necessary, add a splash more vinegar to cook for a long time.

_____

Use a stainless-steel pan to prevent metal contaminating your food and the acid levels corroding the surface. Heavy-based pans are particularly good for chutney, as they conduct a steady heat during the longer cooking time and will help you avoid burning the mixture on the bottom of the pan.

Figure a.

Figure b.

Figure c.

THE POSSIBILITIES

Natural Instincts

Chutney-making is not an exact science and with the basic technique in place you can afford to be creative, playing with a wonderful array of flavours, textures, and colours.

SPICE IT RIGHT

The spice blend used in a chutney can be the difference between a spectacular and a nondescript recipe.

- Allspice, cardamom, cinnamon, clove, cumin, ginger, chilli, mustard seed, and nutmeg is a warming, aromatic combination that works well with tart and sweet flavour profiles. It's also worth experimenting with tamarind, citrus, and fennel.
- Red onion chutney has a natural sweetness that can be overpowering, so add a strong spice such as black mustard seeds to cut through the sugar.
- Try chilli chutney **(fig. a)**, Scotch bonnet chutney with some jerk spices, or sumac and harissa chutney for a Middle Eastern vibe.

Try ... Red onion chutney Finely slice 2kg (4½lb) red onions **(fig. b)** and combine with 1 teaspoon of black mustard seeds and 4–6 sprigs of thyme. Soften the onions in a pan, then add 500ml (16fl oz) cider vinegar and 250g (9oz) sugar. Season and reduce until thick and sticky, then pot into sterilized jars and serve **(fig. c)**.

Figure c.

Figure a.

Figure b.

Figure d.

DRUNKEN CHUTNEYS

Adding 50ml (3 tbsp) alcohol to 500g (1lb 2oz) chutney at the end of the process is a great way to put your own twist on a classic recipe.

- A tomato chutney can be transformed into a Bloody Mary chutney for the perfect "hair-of-the-dog" condiment. Try stirring a spoonful into a Bloody Mary mix and shaking it well for a cocktail with a kick **(fig. d)**.
- Fortified wine and port are great with onion or fig chutney, cider or brandy with apple chutney, or bourbon with cranberry relish.

Try … Bloody Mary chutney Make a tomato chutney by softening 2kg (4½lb) red and green tomatoes **(fig. e)**, 1 head of finely sliced celery, 2 sliced red chillies, 1 tablespoon of grated horseradish, 1 tablespoon of Worcestershire sauce, and 1 teaspoon of freshly ground black pepper in a pan. Add 2 litres (3½ pints) vinegar and 1kg (2¼lb) sugar and reduce. Finish with a generous splash of vodka stirred in at the end.

GO GREEN

Traditional Indian green chutneys are more like fresh, herby pastes, made with minimal cooking.

- Reduce the usual ratio of veg to vinegar to sugar (see Expert Tips, p.39) to 8:2:1 and

Figure e.

drastically reduce the cooking time. Once the vinegar has come to the boil, the chutney is done and ready to eat as soon as it's cool.

- Combinations can be fresh and vibrant with a sweet tang – try coriander with green chilli and coconut, dill and pistachio with lemon, or wild garlic with chilli and cumin.

For me, chutney has a transformative magic, taking fresh fruit and veg and changing their colour, texture, and application. Even the way the relatively simple science can preserve food for months is a wonder.

"

Project 04
JAM, JELLIES, AND SYRUPS
Dollops of fruity sweetness, perfect as a filling or slathered on toast.

SKILL LEVEL Easy.

TIMINGS 20 minutes prep; 40 minutes cooking.

Blackberry jam
Blackberries are naturally high in pectin and therefore perfect for jam-making.

THE SCIENCE

The Gel Network

Jam-making is a classic rite of passage for every cook and a satisfying way to preserve most fruits. To create a traditional jam, fruit and sugar are boiled in large quantities until they reach a soft, spreadable consistency. It's the combination of pectin and acid (which occur naturally in fruits) and added sugar that helps the mixture set – play with the ratios to find your ideal texture. If you find you enjoy jam-making, before you know it you'll be making your own jellies and syrups, too.

PECTIN AND SUGAR

Pectin is a soluble starch found in the cell walls and non-woody parts of all ripe fruit – in the skin, pith, cores, and pips. Without it, jam and jelly wouldn't set, as pectin strands bind together to form a "gel network" that traps the sugar–fruit solution. Some fruits are naturally lower in pectin than others, and to overcome this you can either add citrus peel, pips, or stone fruit as a natural source of pectin, or increase the sugar content, which helps the pectin strands to bind by drawing water away from them. The standard ratio of fruit to sugar for a jam you plan to keep in a cupboard for a season should be 1:1, but if you want a softer, slightly healthier jam to refrigerate, aim for 2:1. For lower-pectin fruit, jam sugar is useful, as it's laced with pectin powder to help jam set, but don't use this with higher-pectin fruit, or you'll end up with jam so solid you could build with it.

ACIDITY

Fruit naturally contains acid, which helps to break down its cell walls, drawing out the pectin and allowing it to do its gelling job properly. If there isn't sufficient acid in the fruit, citric acid is often added to help draw out the pectin and boost the setting process. It also serves as a preservative, because its pH level inhibits the growth of unwanted bacteria. With lower-acidity fruits like peaches or melon, for example, lemon juice (which is high in citric acid) can be added. This not only helps with gelling and preserving; it also gives a well-balanced flavour, with sweet and tart peaks on the tongue.

Gelling agent
Boiling draws out the natural chemical glue in fruits, known as pectin.

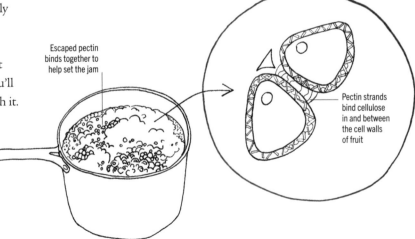

Escaped pectin binds together to help set the jam

Pectin strands bind cellulose in and between the cell walls of fruit

THE PRACTICE

Blackberry Jam

Many jam enthusiasts obsess over their cooking times to achieve the ultimate texture. Personally, I like a loose jam – in Scandinavia they call this a "nearly jam" and use it to make marble swirls in a glossy bowl of yogurt; this tart, jewelled blackberry version is a great example – but if you want a perfectly set jam then take your time and don't overcook the fruit.

Figure a.

Figure b.

Figure c.

MAKES

4 x 290ml (10fl oz) jars

INGREDIENTS

1.8kg (4lb) blackberries
1.5kg (3lb 3oz) caster sugar
2 lemons

EQUIPMENT

tea infuser, muslin, or cheesecloth
heavy-based, stainless-steel
    preserving pan
4 x 290ml (10fl oz) preserving jars,
    sterilized
jam funnel (optional)

Method

01 Add the blackberries and sugar to a bowl and stir well.
Once the berries are evenly covered, leave to macerate
for 1 hour **(fig. a)**.

02 Juice the lemons and retain the pips, which are
particularly high in pectin, for use in the jam.
Transfer the pips to a tea infuser **(fig. b)** or bundle
them in a muslin or cheesecloth parcel tied with string
(so that they are easy to remove later).

03 Place the blackberries, sugar, lemon juice, and pips
in the preserving pan, bring to a rolling boil, and
cook for 15 minutes.

04 Test whether the jam has reached setting point (see
Expert Tips, right). If it hasn't, continue to cook and test
again every 5–10 minutes. When it has reached setting
point, remove the pips and transfer the jam to jars – use
a funnel for ease if you have one. Top each filled jar with
a disc of baking parchment, then seal and label. Keep in
a cool, dark cupboard for 6–12 months. Once opened,
keep refrigerated and use within 2–4 weeks.

EXPERT TIPS

Ensure all jam-making equipment is
sterilized before you start: plunge
jam funnels, spoons, pans, and jars
into boiling water, then dry them in
a warm oven (see pp.8–9).

———

There are various ways to figure out
when your jam has reached setting
point: if using a sugar thermometer,
your jam should be 104–105°C
(219–222°F); alternatively, dip a
wooden spoon into the jam until
fully coated, then allow to cool a
little – the jam should slide slowly
down the spoon and not drop off
unless firmly shaken; or use the
"wrinkle test" – spoon some jam
onto a chilled plate and allow to
cool. When you run your finger
through it, you should make
wrinkles in the jam, leaving a
clear track behind **(fig. c)**.

THE PRACTICE

Marmalade

Marmalade can be a labour of love, but this classic preserve is worth the effort. Your kitchen will smell of perfumed oranges and the result is delightful on toasted brioche, in cakes, or, thanks to its distinctive bitterness, as a glaze for savoury dishes such as ham, salmon, or chicken.

Figure a.

MAKES

4 x 500ml (16fl oz) jars

INGREDIENTS

1.5kg (3lb 3oz) Seville oranges
juice of 2 lemons
2 litres (3½ pints) water
1.5kg (3lb 3 oz) granulated sugar
50ml whisky (optional)

EQUIPMENT

heavy-based, stainless-steel
    preserving pan
fine sieve or muslin bag
4 x 500ml (16fl oz) preserving
    jars, sterilized

Figure b.

Figure c.

Figure d.

Method

01 Start by scalding the whole oranges in a pan of boiling water to remove any wax, then transfer them to a large saucepan with the lemon juice **(fig. a)**.

02 Cover the oranges with water and bring to the boil, reduce the heat, then simmer for 1–2 hours until soft.

03 Carefully remove the oranges with a slotted spoon and set aside to cool **(fig. b)**. Reserve 1.5 litres (2¾ pints) of the water and discard the rest from the pan. Once cool, cut the oranges in half and scoop the pips, pith, and flesh into a fine sieve or muslin bag.

04 Chop the peel into shreds **(fig. c)**, then add to the pan of reserved water with the sugar and squeeze all the juice you can from the pulp in the sieve **(fig. d)** or muslin bag.

05 Stir until the sugar has dissolved and bring to a rolling boil for 10 minutes. Skim off any scum from the surface and test for the setting point (see Expert Tips, p.45).

06 Add the whisky (if using), stir for a final time, then allow to cool slightly so that the peel is distributed evenly and doesn't float to the top. Pour into jars, top with a disc of baking parchment, then seal, label, and keep in a cool, dark cupboard for 6–12 months. Once opened, keep refrigerated and use within 2–4 weeks.

EXPERT TIPS

Pot up marmalade and jam while the jars are still hot from sterilization and the jam is above 85°C (185°F) to kill off unwanted microbes. Covering the top with a disc of baking parchment stops mould from growing on top and the mixture from drying out.

———

If your marmalade or jam ends up too solid, either from overcooking or using jam sugar with a fruit already high in pectin, try adding grape juice to slacken it.

———

Use fresh fruit for marmalade and jam, as overripe fruit contains less pectin. That said, jam is a great way to use up fruit that is soft or bruised – just remember to bump up the pectin level to help it set.

THE POSSIBILITIES

Fruits of Success

Preserving fruit by making jam celebrates traditional recipes but can also be extremely experimental. Try new methods and unusual ingredients to make your own fruit syrup, jelly, and seasonal creations.

SPICED JAM

Once you've mastered a good soft fruit jam, why not experiment with added spices?

- Try cracked black pepper with strawberries, plum jam with cinnamon and star anise, or even blueberry jam with a hint of rosemary.
- Herbs and spices can add a complex background note to jam, which can then be used with savoury dishes - for example, spiced blackberry jam with venison loin (**fig. a**) or strawberry and cracked black pepper jam with cream cheese, balsamic vinegar, and basil.

Try ... Strawberry jam with cracked black pepper Finely chop 1kg (2¼lb) strawberries. Stir in 500g (1lb 2oz) jam sugar with added pectin, then add 2 tablespoons of balsamic vinegar and 1 tablespoon of cracked black pepper. Heat in a preserving pan at a rolling boil for 10–15 minutes until you reach the setting point (see Expert Tips, p.45).

WIBBLE WOBBLE, JELLY ON A PLATE

Making jelly takes a little more patience but follows similar principles to making jam.

- Strain sweetened cooked fruit overnight

> **❝**
>
> *Be bold with your flavours when making jam. Sweetened summer fruits are robust – they can handle punchy spices – though sometimes it pays just to keep it simple: preserve the taste of summer on a humble slice of toast.*
>
> **❞**

Figure a.

Figure b.

Figure c.

Figure d.

through a jelly bag **(fig. b)** or a sieve lined with muslin for a wonderful, clear jelly.

- Once you've poured your jelly into sterilized jars and before it fully sets, add in edible flowers or whole berries and rotate every 15 minutes to suspend them in the jelly.
- Fruit jellies are a sweet counterpoint to winter game or cheese. Try duck with redcurrant jelly or cranberry-glazed chestnuts.

———————

Try ... Redcurrant or cranberry jelly With a 2:1 ratio of fruit to water, cook out the berries in water for an hour, then squish them with a potato masher. Strain overnight through a jelly bag or muslin-lined sieve – without squeezing – then discard the leftover pulp. The next day, add 450g (1lb) sugar for every 600ml (1 pint) juice and bring to the boil. Simmer until you reach the setting point (see Expert Tips, p.45).

A SPOONFUL OF SYRUP

———————

Bottle the medicinal properties of fruit and bolster sauces and cocktails with sweet syrups.

- Seasonal fruits are a rich source of winter vitamins. I often make elderberry **(fig. c)** and rosehip syrups **(fig. d)** in the autumn for their immunity-boosting qualities – both are excellent drizzled over porridge.
- Boil fruit syrups with equal parts vinegar to make shrubs – a tangy addition to cocktails.
- Stir 1 tablespoon of syrup into a gravy or wine reduction to add a fruity sweetness.

———————

Try ... Rosehip syrup Simmer 450g (1lb) fruit with 60ml (2fl oz) water, then strain through a muslin-lined sieve and allow to sit for 30 minutes. Press the solids gently to extract more juice (excessive pressing will create a cloudy syrup), then discard the pulp or use it to make jam. Add 300g (10oz) sugar for every 500ml (16fl oz) strained juice, bring back to the boil, then allow to cool and refrigerate in a sterilized jar for up to 1 month.

"

The sound of jam bubbling in the kitchen is both comforting and nostalgic. I never find making preserves a chore, so I make them little and often, which allows me to forage what's in season from the hedgerows. The result is a larder full of characterful bottles and jars, lined up in colourful splendour.

"

Project 05
FRUIT CURDS
Sweet fruit preserves with a buttery, velvety texture.

SKILL LEVEL Medium:
care is needed when heating
curds to avoid curdling.

TIMINGS 20 minutes
prep; 30 minutes cooking.

Smooth curd
If you are patient and
attentive while cooking
a curd, it should not split.

The Protein Network

A fruit curd is a cooked dish of eggs, sugar, butter, and fruit, in which the egg proteins form a network that traps liquid, creating a smooth, creamy texture. The nature of egg proteins is fragile under heat, though, so stirring continuously during cooking is essential to prevent the protein strands from clumping together and forming a split curd. This delicate balancing act is what gives curds a magnetic power and makes them a pleasure to cook.

THE HEAT EFFECT

Heat encourages the proteins in eggs to bond, triggering the network-building process. When egg proteins are raw, they are tightly coiled, but as they cook and the temperature increases, they start to unravel and link up. Once the egg reaches coagulation temperature, the protein strands bind together, trapping the liquid and building a stable structure. Stirring the mixture continuously during cooking keeps the protein molecules from bonding too tightly, stretching them out so that they form an even mesh, which results in a creamy rather than a solid, lumpy, or "curdled" curd. However, no amount of stirring will prevent the mixture curdling if it is heated too quickly. For that reason, curds are cooked over an indirect heat, in a bowl set over simmering water.

THICKEN AND STABILIZE

The addition of fruit helps preserve the eggs and cuts through the richness to give a sharper flavour. Diluting the eggs with fruit raises the temperature at which coagulation begins, simply because it keeps the protein molecules physically further apart, thus allowing the mixture to heat and thicken more gradually. The use of added sugar also helps to stabilize a curd. The sugar acts as a sort of buffer, coating the egg proteins and therefore increasing the window for heating them before they denature, preventing them from cooking too quickly and becoming unwanted scrambled eggs. Eminent food scientist Harold McGee explains that one tablespoon of sugar is enough to surround each protein molecule in a large egg with a screen of several thousand sucrose molecules.

The curd structure
Stirring over gentle, indirect heat encourages egg proteins to unravel and then link up to form a network that traps liquid.

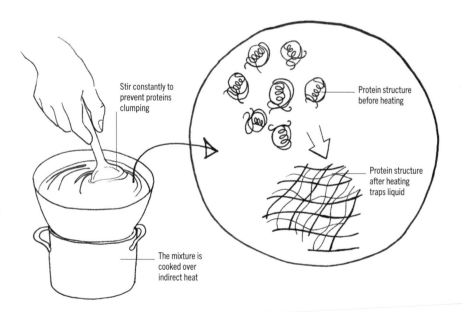

Stir constantly to prevent proteins clumping

The mixture is cooked over indirect heat

Protein structure before heating

Protein structure after heating traps liquid

THE PRACTICE

Lemon Curd

This lemon recipe, with its glowing colour and citrus brightness, is the perfect way to start making curds. The sugar and butter allow you to gently cook the eggs until you have a silky texture popping with flavour. Enjoy these little jars of sunshine spread generously on toast, as a cake filling, with meringue, or marbled in natural yogurt with granola.

Figure a.

Figure b.

Figure c.

MAKES

2 x 120ml (4fl oz) jars

INGREDIENTS

grated zest and juice of 4 unwaxed
    lemons
200g (7oz) caster sugar
100g (3½oz) unsalted butter,
    cut into cubes
3 free-range eggs, plus 1 egg yolk

EQUIPMENT

2 x 120ml (4fl oz) preserving jars,
    sterilized

Method

01 Zest and juice the lemons **(fig. a)**, then add to a
    heatproof bowl with the sugar and butter. Sit the bowl
    over a pan of simmering water, making sure that the
    water doesn't touch the bottom of the bowl. Stir the
    mixture until the butter melts.

02 In a separate bowl whisk the eggs and egg yolk and
    then gradually stir them into the sugary butter
    mixture **(fig. b)**. Stir gently over a low heat until
    all the ingredients are combined.

03 Continue to cook for 10–15 minutes, stirring
    constantly until the mixture is creamy and thick
    enough to coat the back of a spoon.

04 Remove from the heat and set aside to cool. Once
    cooled, pour the curd into glass jars **(fig. c)**, label,
    and keep covered in the fridge. Refrigerate within
    2 hours of making and use within 2 weeks.

EXPERT TIPS

Always use a heatproof bowl over
gently simmering water to heat
your curd – it provides greater
control to prevent boiling,
which will split the mixture.

———

A curd is cooked when it reaches
76°C (170°F), but you'll be able
to tell it's reached the right
consistency when your finger
leaves a clear path through it on
the back of a spoon.

———

Adding a starch such as cornflour
to your fruit curds is like taking out
a "curdling insurance", as starch
molecules absorb heat and get in
the way of the proteins that want
to coagulate. To stabilize a curd,
whisk ½ tsp cornflour into a small
amount of cold water and add to
the curd mixture, stirring briskly
over the heat.

Colourful Curds

Fruit curd is a kitchen skill that invites you to experiment with other flavours, and the creamy richness makes every variation feel like a luxury.

GET FRUITY

A simple curd is an effective way to use up excess fruit, so treat yourself.

- Soften rhubarb over a low heat, then blitz to a purée for the basis of a tart, sweet curd with a fantastic natural pink colour. Some people add pink colouring because they don't think it's bright enough, but I like the understated pastel tones **(fig. a)**. It's great with gooseberry fool and natural yogurt, and in cakes.
- Puréed raspberries or blueberries **(fig. b)** make fruit curds with plenty of acidity and colour, while puréed passion fruit **(fig. c)** makes for a bright and exotic variation.
- Lime makes a better curd than orange, but both are worth trying. Follow the same process as for lemon curd and think about including some zest for more bitterness and acidity.

Try ... Passion fruit curd (fig. d) Put the seeded pulp from 6 passion fruits into a food processor and blitz to loosen the seeds, then strain into a bowl, retaining the solids. Beat together 3 large eggs and 250g (9oz) sugar, then

Figure a.

Figure b.

Figure c.

Figure d.

> *A jar of canary-yellow lemon curd has the ability to light up your fridge when the bulb has gone, and the intoxicating fragrance has a newness like a freshly cleaned kitchen.*

melt 140g (5oz) butter in a heatproof bowl over boiling water and slowly add the sugar and egg mixture. Incorporate the passion fruit juice and, once the mixture is smooth and silky, add in some of the seeds and pulp.

HAPPY COUPLES

Combine two fruits for a more complex curd or experiment with some unexpected flavours.

- Raspberry and lemon, mango and lime, or rhubarb and ginger are classic combinations.
- Add floral notes for a more exciting curd. Edible essential oils or petals (either left in to infuse or strained out) work well. Elderflower and lemon, geranium and orange, or rose and raspberry would be my top tips. All are excellent on toast or for stuffing doughnuts.
- Go for a grown-up version with boozy curds, such as blood orange and bourbon or lemon and gin.

Try ... Lemon curd with gin Add 2 tablespoons of gin to the zest and juice of 2 lemons, 100g (3½oz) sugar and 50g (1¾oz) butter. Then add in 2 large beaten eggs and follow the standard method until the curd thickens.

VEGETABLE CURDS? NO, REALLY

Depending on what's in season and where you live, you may find it worthwhile to experiment with vegetable curds, which can be made by following the same techniques as for fruit curds.

- Have a go at a carrot curd made with spring carrots, which you juice and flavour with a hint of cardamom – this will make a superb layer in a carrot cake.
- For a twist on a red velvet cake, make your own beetroot curd with a pinch of cacao and some fresh raspberry purée.

Project 06
DEHYDRATING

Dried foods for crisp or chewy, intensely flavoursome preservation.

SKILL LEVEL Easy.

TIMINGS 4–12 hours,
depending on produce and
drying method.

Airflow
Slice produce thinly and
space it out on drying
racks to maximize airflow.

THE SCIENCE

Moisture Extraction

Drying food is as simple as it sounds. The basic technique is to thinly slice produce to maximize its surface area so that warm air can pass over it and draw out moisture, thus preventing the growth of unwanted bacteria. The key to effective drying is good air circulation, a constant temperature, and avoiding direct contact with moisture. The result is an intense experience, as the flavours have been packed together closely in the drying process.

PREPARATION

Pretreating produce before dehydrating isn't essential but may help maintain colour, nutrients, and texture. For example, coating apples or pears in lemon juice will avoid browning, since the ascorbic acid creates a barrier between the enzymes in the flesh and the oxygen, slowing the oxidization process that leads to browning. Tough-skinned veg and fruit with a natural protective wax, on the other hand, benefit from blanching. This thermal treatment increases the permeability of cell membranes, which in turn increases the rate of moisture removal. It also destroys the enzymes that would otherwise survive the dehydration process and cause the food to deteriorate. Meat and fish, which have a high moisture content,

generally require brining or dry-salt curing first – the salt draws out much of the moisture by osmosis, speeding up the drying process and inhibiting surface microbes.

CONDITIONS

Controlling the temperature during dehydration is vital. The aim is to remove moisture as quickly as possible without affecting the flavour, texture, and nutritional value of the produce. If the heat is too high, food may case-harden, meaning it will feel dry on the outside, yet moisture will still be trapped inside. If the temperature is too low, the drying time is significantly increased and bacteria may survive and multiply before the food has dried.

Dehydrating apple slices
Maximum airflow, dry air, and a constant temperature are key to controlled moisture removal.

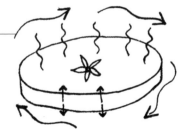

A flow of dry air encourages water to migrate from the interior to the surface, where it evaporates

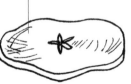

Too much heat can cause case-hardening, when surface sugar "bakes" to form a seal that prevents further moisture loss

A fully dehydrated apple slice will shrink from cellular collapse due to the loss of water content

THE PRACTICE

Dried Apples

With the abundance of apples in autumn, it makes perfect sense not only to preserve the fruit over winter, but also intensify its flavour into a sweet treat for snacking or using in other recipes. Dried apple adds a delicious punch of flavour when used in stuffing and sausages. You can substitute pears, but the dehydrator will need to run for an extra hour, as pears tend to be wetter.

MAKES

800g (1¾lb)

INGREDIENTS

10 dessert apples
(about 1kg/2¼lb)
juice of 1 lemon (optional)

EQUIPMENT

spray bottle (optional)
dehydrator (optional)
silicone baking sheet (optional)
airtight container or freezer bags

Method

01 Peel, core, and slice the apples into rings **(fig. a)** and then segments. (Peeling isn't obligatory – the skin can give the dried pieces a nice, slightly chewy texture. Try them both ways and stick with what you prefer.)

02 If the apple slices start to discolour, use a spray bottle to spritz them with lemon juice before dehydrating or dip them in a solution made with 1 tablespoon of lemon juice and 1 litre (1¾ pints) of water. Drain and dry them well.

03 If using a dehydrator, lay the slices on the drying racks, spaced out to allow good airflow **(fig. b)**, and dry at 50°C (122°F) for 6–8 hours. Alternatively, spread the slices out on a silicone baking sheet and dry in the oven for 5–8 hours at 65°C (149°F) with the fan on and the door slightly ajar to allow moisture to escape. The higher temperature allows for heat loss due to the open door.

04 Remove the slices when they are dry and leathery **(fig. c)**. Aim for 15–20 per cent weight loss. I like them to come out before they become crunchy, but it's up to you.

05 Allow the dried apple slices to cool at room temperature for 30 minutes, then store in a cupboard in an airtight glass jar or sealed bag. They should keep fresh for at least 3–6 months, if not longer.

EXPERT TIPS

Most foods can be dried in a dehydrator or an oven at around 40–50°C (115–122°F), though meat requires a higher temperature of around 70°C (158°F) to kill off unwanted pathogens.

The ideal temperature for storing dried food is 10–16°C (50–61°F). Keep it safe from moisture and insects, in glass jars with tight lids or in vacuum-sealed bags.

To rehydrate dried fruit and veg, cover with boiling water and soak for 5–15 minutes. Alternatively, cover with cool water for 1–2 hours until rehydrated. Dehydrated food absorbs moisture like a sponge, so can come alive when rehydrated in marinades, juices, or alcohol.

Figure a.

Figure b.

Figure c.

THE PRACTICE

Biltong

Originating in South Africa, biltong is dried steak that's been marinated in spices and vinegar for extra flavour and to help preserve it. To avoid any surface microbes on the meat, it's always best to cure it first, but avoid over-salted biltong, which can be unpalatable. You can try the same technique with goat, venison, lamb, or even rabbit.

MAKES

750g (1lb 10oz)

INGREDIENTS

1kg (2¼lb) beef skirt
   or flank
2 tsp salt
2 tbsp brown sugar
4 tbsp cider vinegar
1 tbsp chilli flakes
1 tbsp cracked black pepper
1 tbsp coriander seeds

EQUIPMENT

dehydrator (optional)
500ml (16fl oz) preserving
   jar, sterilized (optional)

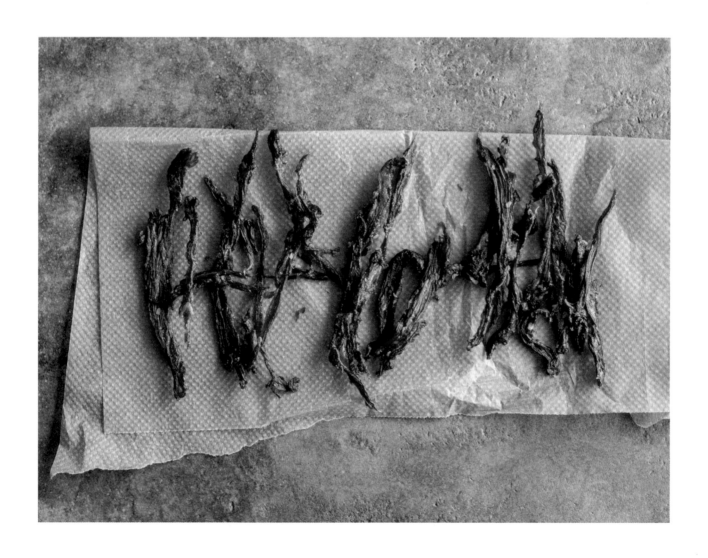

Method

01 Using a very sharp knife, slice the beef along the grain into long strips **(fig. a)**. (I sometimes freeze the meat a little first so that I can slice very thinly and often use a sashimi knife for thinner strips.) Trim off any sinew or fat, as this doesn't dry as easily.

02 Mix your cure using the remaining ingredients and massage into the beef strips. Arrange the meat in a dish and cover with the remaining cure **(fig. b)**. Leave covered in the fridge for 4–6 hours, turning the meat and massaging it again every couple of hours.

03 Remove the meat from the cure, shake off the seasoning, and pat dry with a paper towel. If using, set your dehydrator to around 68–71°C (154–160°F) – the maximum on most models – and lay the strips on the drying racks, allowing plenty of space between them **(fig. c)**.

04 If you don't have a dehydrator, dry the beef in your oven at 70°C (158°F), with the fan on and the door slightly ajar to allow moisture to escape. Hang the beef strips between the oven racks using cocktail sticks, with a tray beneath to catch any dripping fat.

05 Dehydrate for 4–8 hours. Aim for 35–50 per cent weight loss, depending on how dry you like your biltong. Personally, I like a slightly wetter, leathery texture, rather than it being so dry that it's dusty when rubbed between your fingers.

06 Store in baking parchment or a preserving jar in a cupboard for 4–6 days, or keep sealed in the fridge for 2–4 weeks. The surface of the biltong may turn white in patches, but don't be alarmed by this; it's likely to be the salt from your marinade dehydrating.

EXPERT TIPS

A dehydrator is a wonderful artisan kitchen gadget to own and can be used for drying all sorts of food. I recommend investing in one if you want to reduce your food waste and make your own healthy snacks.

———

Alternatively, try building your own dehydrator. Take an old cupboard or fridge, install some wire shelving, then plug in an electric fan at the bottom. Cut 5 holes in the top of the dehydrator, the same size as a wine cork, and moderate the airflow by popping in corks to restrict or increase the flow as needed.

Figure a.

Figure b.

Figure c.

THE POSSIBILITIES

Gourmet Dehydrating

Dehydrating is probably the oldest preserving method there is, and the beauty of this relatively simple process is that you can have a go at drying almost anything.

FORAGED FAVOURITES

When a growing season is fleeting, you want to preserve those precious tastes in as many ways as you can.

- Make instant dashi stock from dried nettles, seaweed, and ceps. Add miso and boiling water with noodles for an umami-rich broth.
- Make intensely flavoured powders by grinding dried produce such as wild garlic in a spice blender (see p.26).
- With such a short wild fruit season, I like to dehydrate blackberries, haw berries, and alpine strawberries, then blitz for a fruity crumb **(fig. a)** to use in granola and herbal teas.

THE SEA, THE SEA

All kinds of seafood can be dehydrated, and the results can be wonderful. For an added layer of food safety, cure the fish before drying. This removes excess water and helps provide a hostile environment for unwanted microbes.

- Try making your own salmon biltong, swordfish jerky, or mojama (Mediterranean salted and dried tuna) thinly sliced and served with almonds and olive oil.
- Dehydrate fish skin **(fig. b)** by blanching for 30 seconds, then drying at 45°C (113°F) for 4–6 hours until crisp. Then fry in hot oil for a few seconds so it puffs into a delicious crisp.

Figure a.

Figure b.

Figure c.

Figure d.

FLAVOURED SALTS

Sprinkle fragrant or spicy salt blends over a dish or use as the base of an aromatic cure.

- Dried calendula and rose petals make incredible floral salts **(fig. c)** for seasoning lamb or melted chocolate.
- Blitz dried chillies into a fine flake and combine with sea salt for a spicy sprinkle.
- Dried seaweed flakes **(fig. d)** are excellent for making your own seaweed butter (see p.110).

FRUIT AND VEG CRISPS

Fruit and veg crisps are a healthy treat and can add a great textural element to meals.

- Reduce food waste by drying out apple peel into crunchy crisps that are delicious on a bowl of yogurt or chopped into granola.
- Plate up kale crisps with preserved lemons, anchovy, calendula petals, and fresh mint **(fig. e)**. Sprinkle with olive oil and sea salt for a mouthwatering, mineral-rich dish.

Try ... Kale crisps Blanch 150g (5½oz) kale in boiling water for a few seconds, then plunge into a bowl of ice-cold water to lock in the colour and flavour. Remove the woody stems and veins, then chop the kale into crisp-sized pieces. Massage with a drizzle of oil, and try adding some fermented chilli and garlic powder (see p.26) for a special treat. Spread out evenly on a rack in your dehydrator at 40°C (115°F) or on a baking sheet lined with parchment in an oven at 50°C (122°F) for 3–5 hours. Check after 3 hours and every 30 minutes or so thereafter until crunchy. Store in an airtight container and consume within 1–2 weeks.

Figure e.

Project 07
VINEGAR

An acidic, gut-friendly condiment to sharpen or preserve.

SKILL LEVEL Medium:
optimum conditions for
the fermenting mother
need to be controlled.

TIMINGS 5 minutes prep;
3–8 weeks for maturing.

Vinegar mother
It's a sign that vinegar is
ready when the mother
sinks to the bottom.

THE SCIENCE

Acetous Fermentation

I first made vinegar by mistake, and in enormous quantities, when I was fermenting a large barrel of cider on the farm where I grew up. A bung was not secured properly so the cider was exposed to the air, meaning that, on contact with oxygen, the visiting natural bacteria fermented the alcohol into acetic acid. The error wasn't all bad, though, as the resulting cider vinegar proved extremely useful for that year's chutney-making. I now try to make my own cider vinegar on purpose in my kitchen at home.

MOTHER CULTURE

Alcohol is converted to vinegar in a process called acetous fermentation, whereby the *Acetobacter aceti* strain of bacteria feed on the sugars and alcohol and create acetic acid as a by-product, which gives vinegar its tangy, mouth-puckering taste. The cellulose molecules in the alcohol and vinegar bacteria form a live culture that will develop as a healthy jelly-like layer on the surface, called the "mother". It'll also be apparent as cloudy wisps in unpasteurized vinegar. The culture responsible for the acetous fermentation of alcoholic liquids such as wine or cider is a living thing and has been proven to be beneficial for our gut health if vinegar is consumed raw and unpasteurized.

ENVIRONMENT

Unlike the lacto-bacteria of sour pickles, vinegar bacteria need oxygen to survive and thrive. They are also fussy about temperature; 5–10°C (40–50°F) can make all the difference to their growth speed and if fermentation will take place at all. The efficiency window for vinegar bacteria is narrow: 25–30°C (77–86°F). The productivity curve slowly ramps up as it reaches the optimum temperature but falls off a cliff once it goes beyond. The final stage of the process is ageing the vinegar. The complex chemistry that occurs during maturation is the slow conversion of acetic acid into smaller esters – molecules that impart awesome levels of flavour into the vinegar.

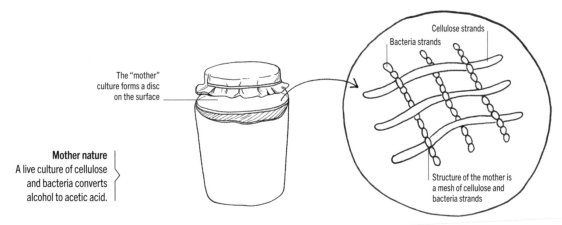

The "mother" culture forms a disc on the surface

Cellulose strands

Bacteria strands

Mother nature
A live culture of cellulose and bacteria converts alcohol to acetic acid.

Structure of the mother is a mesh of cellulose and bacteria strands

THE PRACTICE

Cider Vinegar

As with sourdough and kombucha, the key to making a good vinegar is to be a well-behaved child and look after your mother. I use vinegar in almost all my cooking to add sharp notes and permeate heavier dishes with a palate-cleansing clarity, so for me, it's essential to use a high-quality natural vinegar. You can buy unpasteurized vinegar as a "starter" for the bacteria culture, which speeds up the process and cuts out much of the hassle compared to spontaneous fermentation.

MAKES

1.5 litres (2¾ pints)

INGREDIENTS

1 litre (1¾ pints) cider
100ml (3½fl oz) raw unpasteurized
  cider vinegar

EQUIPMENT

1.5-litre (2¾-pint) wide-neck
  glass jar, sterilized
muslin or cheesecloth
2 x 750ml (1¼-pint) glass bottles,
  sterilized

Method

01 Pour the cider into a glass jar **(fig. a)**.

02 Add the raw cider vinegar and stir well – the mother culture will kill off any bad bacteria during the fermentation process.

03 Cover the jar with a square of muslin or cheesecloth and hold it in place with string or an elastic band, so that it is sealed but air can still flow through **(fig. b)**.

04 Stir daily for the first few weeks and soon enough you will find the mother starting to form on the surface of your vinegar. Leave the cider in a warm place, at 25–30°C (77–86°F), to slowly ferment and turn into vinegar for the next 3 months.

05 Once the vinegar has reached a suitable tanginess for your taste, strain it through layers of muslin or cheesecloth to remove most of the mother, preventing further fermentation, and pour into glass bottles. Retain the mother of vinegar and start on the next batch or keep it stored in vinegar until you want to make more.

EXPERT TIPS

You can make vinegar by simply leaving cider open in your kitchen for long enough, but you risk letting all the wrong types of bacteria into the mix. I prefer batch fermentation with a mother culture.

During fermentation, store your vinegar in sealed glass containers in a warm cupboard, rather than a cool larder where fermentation could slow down or cease completely. If stored correctly, vinegar can age almost indefinitely – Chinese vinegars for 3–6 years; balsamic and sherry vinegar for 12–25 years.

If fermenting in a metal container, only use stainless steel, which won't corrode from the acid. I use stainless steel or glass jars so that I can see the progress of my vinegar.

Figure a.

Figure b.

THE POSSIBILITIES

Tangy Treats

A drizzle of flavoured vinegar can lift a dish much like gravy does a roast and will help you capture seasonality like an Impressionist painter.

FRUITY FLAVOURS

Vinegars can acquire an array of flavours by steeping fruit in them after fermentation.

- Rhubarb and plums make delicious, brightly coloured vinegars. They are particularly good with ginger, served with stir-fries and soy-glazed tofu.
- Strawberry with chamomile **(fig. a)** is extremely fragrant and works very well with sea bass or in an Eton Mess, where it cuts through the sweetness.
- Some of my favourite fruity flavours are figs **(fig. b)** or raspberries added to home-made vinegar just before bottling. These are then superb when used in dressings, marinades, and pickles.

———

Try ... Raspberry vinegar Crush 500g (1lb 2oz) raspberries with a fork, then steep in 500ml (16fl oz) white wine vinegar. Allow to infuse overnight and the next day strain the juice into a stainless-steel pan. Simmer with 75g (2½oz) sugar for 5–10 minutes. Pour into a sterilized bottle and use to deglaze a pan when cooking venison loin or liver. This vinegar is also delicious with a rocket, walnut, and blue cheese salad, whisked into olive oil as a fruity dressing.

Figure a.

Figure b.

Figure c.

VARIETY IS THE SPICE OF LIFE

Add herbs, spices, and aromatics, and vary the alcohol base, for softer layers of flavour.

- Anise profiles such as tarragon work well with cider vinegar; lemongrass and rose petal with white wine vinegar. Try saffron vinegar for a punch of colour and spice.
- Almost any unfortified alcohol can be used as a base for making vinegar, from real ale to red wine to champagne. You can even use the alcohol produced by leftover scraps of fruit.

Try ... Compost vinegar Make your own apple vinegar using scraps, peelings, and cores. Cover with a 1:2 solution of sugar to water and leave to ferment for 1–2 weeks at warm room temperature. Once the bubbling slows down, you can convert the fruit alcohol into acetic acid by straining the liquid into a wide-necked glass container covered with muslin. Store at room temperature away from direct sunlight for 3–6 months. A mother will form on the surface, then sink to the bottom once it's finished converting alcohol to vinegar.

BOOSTING UMAMI

Vinegar can be accused of being too mono in its taste dimension, but you can combat this by infusing the vinegar base with umami flavours.

- Create dressings with real depth by using black garlic **(fig. c)** for a balsamic-rich flavoured vinegar, or use the Japanese-inspired method of enriching vinegars with seaweed and dashi.
- If ageing vinegar, you can add oak chips or dried herbs, but do so sparingly, as the flavours will intensify over time. Boil the oak chips first to reduce the harsh tannins and mellow the flavour.

Once you've explored the possibilities of flavoured vinegar, you'll find it hard to use straight vinegar as a condiment ever again.

DRINKS

Project 08
FERMENTED SOFT DRINKS
Refreshing beverages with a slight lactic tang and sweet balance.

SKILL LEVEL Easy: maintaining mother health is the only challenge.

TIMINGS 2–4 weeks to establish the culture; 7–10 days for initial fermentation; 1–3 days for secondary fermentation.

Kombucha bases
A wide variety of teas, and even fruit juices, can be used as the base for kombucha.

THE SCIENCE

Probiotics

In the last decade fermented soft drinks such as kombucha have taken the drinks world by storm. Such drinks rely on two symbiotic fermentation processes working in tandem: yeast converting sugar to alcohol, and bacteria then converting that alcohol to acetic acid. The research is inconclusive, but it's generally acknowledged that the live probiotic bacteria contribute to better gut health, which has undoubtedly increased the appeal of these drinks. That they taste fantastic is enough motivation for me.

BACTERIAL FERMENTATION

Fermented drinks rely on a living culture to encourage the acetic acid bacteria to multiply. The yeasts in these cultures eat the sugars, such as lactose and glucose, in the drink base and produce ethanol (alcohol), which is then converted by the bacteria into acetic acid. This produces carbon dioxide, resulting in refreshing pop drinks with a slight fizzy tang. The pH of kombucha decreases due to this acid-producing mechanism during fermentation, leading to the slightly sharp, sour flavour. This also inhibits the growth of unwanted organisms and favours the acetic acid bacteria, which thrive in low-pH acidic environments. Unlike lactobacilli, acetic acid bacteria also require exposure to oxygen to thrive and do their job of converting alcohol.

LIVING CULTURES

The living culture fermenting kombucha is known as a SCOBY (symbiotic colony of bacteria and yeasts). This is a biofilm that thrives on sweetened, caffeinated black or green tea, sugar, and filtered water. The SCOBY grows as a cellulose floating disc, and as it brews, the tea ferments and the yeasts turn sugar into alcohol, which the bacteria then convert into acetic acid, providing its tangy taste as well as helping to preserve it. For ginger beer, root beer, and other fermented sodas, a ginger bug made with ginger, water, and sugar that ferments due to the wild yeasts in the surrounding environment provides the starter culture.

Tea fermentation
Acetic acid bacteria create microbial cellulose, onto which the culture of bacteria and yeast adheres. Yeast feeds off the sugars in tea to create alcohol, which the bacteria feed on and convert to acetic acid.

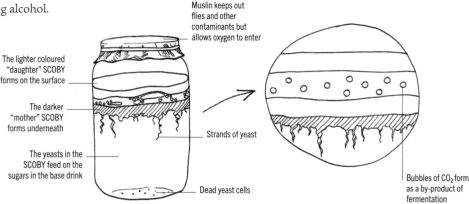

Muslin keeps out flies and other contaminants but allows oxygen to enter

The lighter coloured "daughter" SCOBY forms on the surface

The darker "mother" SCOBY forms underneath

The yeasts in the SCOBY feed on the sugars in the base drink

Strands of yeast

Dead yeast cells

Living culture
The SCOBY is a floating cellulose disc that ferments the base drink.

Bubbles of CO_2 form as a by-product of fermentation

THE PRACTICE

Ginger Beer

Ginger beer is a refreshing probiotic drink that is made using a starter of sugar, root ginger, and water, known as a ginger bug. Fermentation is triggered by the wild yeasts that float in the air and live on the ginger itself, and the result is a lovely cocktail that is also great for digestion. A ginger bug can also be used for tonics, root beer, or even probiotic lemonade.

MAKES

600ml (1 pint)

INGREDIENTS

For the ginger bug starter

50g (1¾oz) fresh root ginger, plus 5–6 tsp chopped root ginger for daily feeding

zest and juice of ½ lemon

2 tsp cane sugar, plus 5–6 tsp for daily feeding

75ml (2½fl oz) water, plus 5–6 tsp for daily feeding

For the ginger beer

500ml (16fl oz) apple juice or green tea sweetened with 5 tbsp raw cane sugar

EQUIPMENT

pestle and mortar

muslin or cheesecloth

750ml (1¼-pint) flip-top glass bottle, sterilized

Figure a.

Method

01 Peel your root ginger and cut into thin slices, then bruise the slices well by crushing them with a pestle and mortar.

02 Place the ginger in a glass or bowl and add the lemon zest, juice, and sugar **(fig. a)**.

03 Add 75ml (2½fl oz) warm water (enough to cover the ginger and dissolve the sugar) **(fig. b)**. If you have a little ginger beer from a previous ginger bug batch, add this to kick-start the process. Cover the glass with a square of muslin or cheesecloth and secure with a piece of string or an elastic band to protect the culture but allow airflow **(fig. c)**.

04 Leave the culture to develop on your kitchen work surface for 24 hours at 15–25°C (59–77°F), then for 5–6 days afterwards add a little of the extra root ginger, water, and sugar every day – 1 teaspoon of each at a time should be sufficient.

05 When your ginger bug starts to bubble and smell of wild yeasts, it's ready to use. Strain the bug, discarding the root ginger, and mix the 100ml (3½fl oz) ginger bug liquid with the 500ml (16fl oz) apple juice or sweetened green tea. If you want to make a more refreshing ginger beer, then use a lighter ginger infusion: 100ml (3½fl oz) ginger bug with 1 litre (1¾ pints) fruit juice or tea sweetened with 50g (1¾ oz) sugar.

06 Pour into a flip-top bottle, leaving a 1–2cm (½–¾in) space at the top for the ginger beer to ferment, then seal and store at 21°C (70°F) for up to 48 hours before transferring to the fridge. Enjoy within 1–2 months.

EXPERT TIPS

It's a good idea to start your ginger bug in the summer when it's warm and there are lots of natural yeasts floating about. Put the bug outside on a sunny day to get it started.

———

Keep your ginger bug out on a kitchen surface if feeding it daily. If you want a slower fermentation to better suit your routine, keep it in the fridge and feed once a week with 1 tablespoon of grated root ginger, 1 tablespoon of water, and 1 tablespoon of sugar. If kept in the fridge, bring it to room temperature before feeding and allow to sit for a few hours to ferment before returning to the fridge.

———

Introduce fermented drinks into your diet incrementally if not used to them to avoid tummy upset.

Figure b.

Figure c.

MAKES

800ml (1¼ pints)

INGREDIENTS

800ml (1¼ pints) green tea,
    brewed with 10g (¼oz)
    loose-leaf tea or 4 tea bags
50g (1¾oz) raw cane sugar
kombucha mother or SCOBY
    (available to buy online, or get
    one from a friend who has
    already made kombucha)

EQUIPMENT

1-litre (1¾-pint) wide-rimmed
    preserving jar, sterilized
muslin or cheesecloth
tea strainer or sieve
1-litre (1¾-pint) sealable glass
    bottle(s), sterilized

THE PRACTICE

Kombucha

Kombucha is a cool, refreshing fermented tea that improves gut flora and is
packed with B vitamins, vitamin C, and antioxidant-rich polyphenols. For
best results the tea should be caffeinated, as the SCOBY feeds on the caffeine
and other nutrients in the tea, which boosts healthy growth, but you can try
fermenting with other herbal blends and adding extra flavours.

Method

01 Brew a strong green tea at 85°C (185°F) **(fig. a)**, add the sugar and stir to dissolve, then allow to infuse until the tea has cooled to room temperature.

02 Remove the tea leaves or bags using a strainer or sieve, pour the tea into a large jar, and place the kombucha mother or SCOBY on top **(fig. b)**. It may sink at first, but once the ferment has established, the carbonation will help it float to the top, forming a natural seal.

03 Cover the jar with muslin or cheesecloth and secure with an elastic band to allow the gases to escape during fermentation and oxygen to reach the bacteria **(fig. c)**.

04 Store at room temperature – aim for 18–22°C (64–72°F) – for 7–10 days until the tea tastes good. It should have a slight fizz, a pleasant sour tang, and a balance of sweetness and acidity. Don't worry if the occasional batch falls short of the mark (if you get the balance wrong or ferment for too long, it can taste vinegary). For a sweeter kombucha, add some fresh berries or a teaspoon of sugar for a secondary fermentation. Alternatively, next time add a little more sugar or shorten the fermenting time.

05 To harvest, strain the kombucha through a sieve into a bottle, seal, and store in the fridge for 1–2 weeks. Enjoy chilled. You can get a second fermentation in the bottle if there are still sugars present, so check the pressure daily and release any build-up of carbon dioxide.

06 Retain the SCOBY in your original kombucha jar and make more of the same tea base – or try a different base – to keep the SCOBY alive and fermenting.

EXPERT TIPS

With a couple of batches on the go, you'll soon have kombucha coming out of your ears! Take steps to slow it down a bit by storing somewhere cool. I also share a few mother cultures with friends and family to kick-start their bucha habit.

———

Drink or pour off some kombucha each week, then top up with fresh tea for a continuous fermentation. Repeat this recipe to keep the SCOBY healthy, but use half-measures if only topping up. A sign of whether the mother needs more tea and sugar is if it starts to sink to the bottom of the jar.

Figure a.

Figure b.

Figure c.

Bubbling Buchas

Straight-up kombucha – tangy, sweet, and subtly bitter – is tough to beat, but like most artisan crafts, once you've got a good grasp of the basics, there are no limits.

MOTHER BLENDS

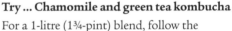

Kombucha is a great way to use up stewed tea leaves. After perfecting the fermentation of green tea to feed your SCOBY, move on to other kinds of tea for a variety of fizzy kombucha.

- Try caffeinated black tea with raspberries for a full, fruity flavour. Alternatively, blend chamomile and green tea for a more floral ferment or use a stronger herbal or botanical infusion alongside the caffeinated tea.

- Other caffeinated teas such as jasmine, Assam white tea, or even a smoky lapsang souchong can be fermented.
- You can produce kombucha with caffeine-free teas like rooibos, hibiscus, raspberry leaf, or nettle, but your SCOBY won't like it if that's what you do batch after batch, as it feeds on caffeine. Reintroducing caffeine occasionally will therefore ensure a healthy culture.

Try … Chamomile and green tea kombucha
For a 1-litre (1¾-pint) blend, follow the standard process for making kombucha, but start by brewing 500ml (16fl oz) of each tea made with a strong infusion and see if you like the flavours. You can then increase the chamomile ratio if you wish, as long as you return to the higher green tea ratio every 2–3 batches to keep the SCOBY healthy.

Figure a.

Figure b.

Figure c.

Figure d.

POST-FERMENT FLAVOURS

After brewing a batch of kombucha and straining off the fermented liquid, you can add huge amounts of flavour.

- Options that are worth trying include: lemon and oregano **(fig. a)**, mint and raspberries **(figs b and c)**, blueberries **(fig. d)**, root ginger, strawberries and basil, apple and cinnamon, a virgin mojito with mint and lime, or a supercharged turmeric kombucha.
- Try throwing in foraged flavours like pineapple weed, seabuckthorn, or gorse.
- Experiment with mild spices like cardamom, star anise, or juniper. Dried or frozen fruit can be added and vegetables such as beetroot, carrot, or cucumber work well. For something darker, try coffee, charcoal, or cacao powder.

FIZZING FERMENTS

Enjoy the possibilities of extra-fizzy bucha.

- Taking a delicately fermented kombucha, adding sugar for a secondary fermentation, and then bottling it creates a bubbly pop like no other. Ensure that it's left in a warm place for faster fermentation.

- Fruit juice is excellent added to kombucha for a secondary fermentation. Use freshly squeezed juice or fruit purée packed with natural sugars and enzymes for a lively fizz.
- Use sturdy flip-top bottles that won't explode under pressure or let gases escape.

> ❝
>
> *Experimenting with carbonated ferments, you find yourself intimately involved with the drinks – making small adjustments to temperature or sugar levels – which bloom with life.*
>
> ❞

Project 09
CIDER

A sweet-sharp alcoholic beverage of fermented apples.

SKILL LEVEL Medium:
it can be challenging to
balance the levels of acidity
and sweetness to taste.

TIMINGS 30 minutes
prep; 1–2 weeks fermenting;
2 weeks–4 months maturing.

Home-made cider
Create a blend that
has a tannic back note
balanced by sweetness.

THE SCIENCE

Ethanol Fermentation

During the cider-making process, the natural sugars in apple juice are converted to alcohol by yeast, and in addition the malic acid is converted to lactic acid and carbon dioxide, which rounds the flavour and reduces the acidity of the cider. The most important factor that shapes a cider, however, is the blend of apples used – perfecting the balance of sweet and bitter notes can come down to years of trial and error.

AVOIDING OXIDATION

The key to successful apple fermentation is cleanliness and preventing air from returning to your fermentation. The naturally occurring wild yeasts in apple juice convert sugars such as glucose and fructose into cellular energy by ethanol fermentation, producing alcohol (ethanol) and carbon dioxide as by-products. It is essential that the carbon dioxide can escape the fermentation demijohn but that oxygen can't get into it; this is to avoid oxidation and the introduction of unwanted bacteria into the cider, otherwise it can develop unpleasant flavours and turn into vinegar. For this reason, an airlock is fitted to the demijohn during fermentation, and after racking off, the cider is stored in sterilized, airtight bottles.

SWEETNESS, ACIDITY, AND TANNINS

The process of malolactic fermentation converts the malic acid in apples into lactic acid and carbon dioxide. This conversion lowers the overall acidity of the cider and provides a fuller flavour. Some cider-makers add malic acid after fermentation has finished to increase the acidity and modify the flavour. Another strong influence over the taste of cider is the level of tannins. These are soluble polyphenolic compounds found in many plants and foods, including grapes, dark chocolate, and apples. They not only contain beneficial antioxidants but add a bitter, astringent quality to the brew. Some of the finest ciders are made using bittersweet apples that are high in tannins and sugar but low in acid, such as Dabinetts, though sweeter dessert apples can also bring great success.

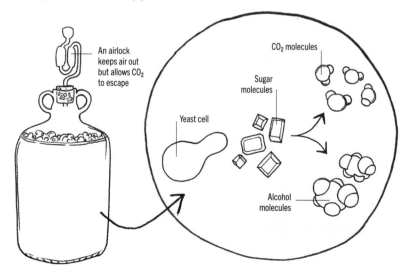

An airlock keeps air out but allows CO_2 to escape

CO_2 molecules

Sugar molecules

Yeast cell

Alcohol molecules

Ethanol fermentation
Yeast cells multiply by feeding on sugar, creating alcohol and carbon dioxide as by-products.

THE PRACTICE

Scrumpy Cider

For scrumpy, aim for a selection of apples that blend each flavour quarter: sharp, sweet, bittersweet, and bitter-sharp. That said, it's fine to use whatever apples you've got, but a mix of varieties is best. For the best chance of a tasty drop, juice a small batch of your apples and taste-test the combination first to understand the ratios before making gallons of cider.

MAKES

2.5 litres (4 pints)

INGREDIENTS

4kg (8¾lb) apples (mixed varieties: Dabinett, Somerset Red, and Yarlington Mill are bittersweet; Cox's Orange Pippin, Golden Delicious, and Worcester Pearmain are sweet; Royal Russet and Herefordshire Costard are sharp; Kingston Black, Foxwhelp, and Porter's Perfection are bitter-sharp)
¼ teaspoon cider yeast (optional)
½ Campden tablet, crushed in a little warm water or juice (optional – see Expert Tips, opposite)

EQUIPMENT

juicer or food processor
hydrometer (optional – see Expert Tips, opposite)
demijohn, sterilized
fermentation airlock
section of drainpipe or syphoning tube
3 x 1-litre (1¾-pint) glass bottles, sterilized
funnel

Method

01 Chop the apples so you can fit them into your juicer or food processor **(fig. a)** and discard any brown bits. Juice the apples **(fig. b)**, including the peel, core, and pips, and remove any lumps by passing through a sieve. If you have a hydrometer (see Expert Tips, right), use it to measure the gravity of the liquid before fermentation.

02 Pour the apple juice into a clean demijohn. At this stage you can add commercial cider yeast, as per the packet instructions, to speed up fermentation, but I like to let the wild yeasts do their job. Secure an airlock on top and half fill with water to prevent airflow but allow the gas from the fermentation to escape **(fig. c)**.

03 Leave the juice to ferment in the demijohn at 15–20°C (59–68°F) for 1–2 weeks, checking regularly that the temperature remains fairly constant.

04 If you're using commercial yeast, the cider should be ready to rack off after 3–4 weeks. For wild yeasts it's closer to 3 months before fermentation ceases and the bubbles stop being produced. At this stage you can add half a Campden tablet to kill off any unwanted yeasts and reduce the likelihood of the cider spoiling after fermentation (see Expert Tips, right), though I prefer to leave the scrumpy as a living thing that is slightly less predictable but more natural.

05 To rack off the alcohol, insert a pipe or tube just above the sediment in the demijohn and suck the cider upwards. Lower the pipe, pour into a jug, and decant into bottles using a funnel. If using a hydrometer, take a second reading to calculate the alcohol level.

06 Keep at room temperature for 3–6 weeks before enjoying chilled. You can drink it sooner, but the longer you let the cider mature, the better it'll taste.

EXPERT TIPS

Campden tablets are sulphur-based sterilizing tablets sometimes used to kill off bad yeasts while encouraging the good ones for fermentation. Add 1 tablet per gallon if doing a wild ferment.

———

Hydrometers measure the specific gravity of a liquid and indicate the sugar content and potential alcohol level of cider. Float the hydrometer in a tall glass container of juice and take a reading. Take a second reading after fermentation and subtract from the initial reading to give the alcohol level.

Figure a.

Figure b.

Figure c.

"

The artisan kitchen isn't complete without a home-made drink to pair with the food on your menu. Making a gallon of mulled cider for an autumn gathering or serving chilled fizzy kombucha on a hot summer's day will elevate the whole experience of sharing food.

"

Beyond Scrumpy

For purists, anything other than a natural scrumpy just isn't real cider, but I always feel empowered to experiment with my own ideas once I've learnt an artisanal skill.

ALTERNATIVE CIDERS

Cider doesn't have to be a flat drink reserved for blustery autumn nights.

- Fizzy cider is fantastic as an alternative to champagne and sparkling wine (fig. a). With the right balance of sweetness, it makes a lovely dessert wine or goes well with fish.
- Perry is made in a similar way to cider but with pears. Its sweet, floral notes work well with blue cheese, walnuts, and pork.
- Fruity versions are excellent for poaching fruit or as a base cocktail mixer. Try adding strawberries and fruit juice at fermentation.

Try ... Fizzy cider Take 4.5 litres (8 pints) cider and rack off at a specific gravity of 1.003 (use a hydrometer to measure this, see p.85) into five 750ml (1¼-pint) heavy-duty champagne bottles. Allow the cider to finish fermenting and mature in the bottle. The carbon dioxide will dissolve to produce bubbles when the bottle is opened.

FLAVOURED CIDER

I was always a Cornish sceptic when it came to flavoured cider, but I've since been converted.

- I once tried a cider with elderflower that blew my mind. It was floral and sweet, with a freshness that offset the bitter-sharp base.

Figure a.

Figure b.

Figure c.

> **"**
>
> *Craft brewers are now reinventing classic farmhouse cider with innovative blends and exciting flavoured options, producing vintage bottle-fermented cider with all the depth of flavour of a good champagne.*
>
> **"**

Figure d.

- Try adding pear juice and ginger after fermentation, or add gin-infused sloe berries at the point of fermentation, straining them out after 48 hours, for a "slider" **(fig. b)**.
- Infusing blackberries **(fig. c)** post-fermentation makes a bramble cider that is delicious when reduced into a sticky sauce to pair with pheasant or venison, or as a syrup in a hearty winter berry cobbler.

Try ... Elderflower cider Pour the juice of 8kg (17lb 8oz) apples into a demijohn with 6–8 big elderflower heads and leave for 36–48 hours to infuse. Strain, then add 1 teaspoon of champagne yeast. Ferment in the demijohn, sealed with an airlock, at 15–20°C (59–68°F) for 8 weeks or until fermentation ceases. Rack off and add 1½ teaspoons of sugar per litre for a fizzy elderflower cider. Transfer to champagne bottles, store horizontally for 10 days, then refrigerate for 24 hours before opening.

WINTER WARMERS

Even an average scrumpy can be improved with the addition of mulling spices.

- Warm sweet cider slowly on the stove with orange peel, cinnamon bark, cloves, allspice berries, root ginger, star anise, and a splash of apple brandy for some added warmth **(fig. d)**.
- Farmhouse cider is very good in a winter hot toddy with whisky and honey.
- Reduce cider to a syrupy consistency and add 1 teaspoon to a chai latte for fruity depth.

Project 10
FLAVOURED SPIRITS

Heady liquors infused with fruit and botanicals.

SKILL LEVEL Easy.

TIMINGS 15 minutes prep; 4 weeks–3 months maturation period, checking regularly.

Fruity infusions
Sloes and blackberries impart wonderful colour and flavour to alcohol.

THE SCIENCE

Alcoholic Infusions

I haven't yet been able to justify setting up a pot still in my kitchen to start experimenting with my own spirits, so the next best thing is to visit my network of local artisan brewers, who let me play with theirs. Flavoured spirits are distilled liquors, high-purity alcohols, and fortified wines that have had fruits, nuts, and botanicals added to macerate and infuse for an extra taste dimension. They make fantastic gifts for friends and family.

INFUSION

Immersing herbs, spices, or fruit in a solvent such as alcohol allows the chemical flavour compounds to leach out from the botanicals' cells. Motion, heat, and pressure can all be used to increase the rate of extraction by bruising cell membranes to release the flavour molecules. Traditionally, however, to infuse spirits with flavour the crucial ingredient is time. The process involves combining fruit and botanicals with a spirit in a large glass jar, sealing it, and then waiting either weeks or months while the soluble flavours leach out of the plant and into the liquor. Creating motion by either turning or shaking the container on a regular basis agitates the ingredients to aid the melding and infusion process.

PRESSURE AND HEAT

The standard infusion process is slow, so mixologists have developed ways to force the ingredients and liquid together to infuse more quickly. One way is to use a cream-whipper or siphon gun to pressurize an infusion with a nitrous oxide cartridge. The pressure pushes the liquid and solid together, and, as the pressure is released, pulls them apart again; this movement disrupts the cells of the solid ingredient, aiding the flavour extraction. The other method for rapid infusion is to heat it no higher than 77.5°C (171.5°F) – just below the boiling point of alcohol. The heat generates kinetic energy, which agitates the flavour compounds and makes them more volatile, allowing them to leach into the alcohol more easily.

Flavour extraction
Volatile chemical compounds form the main flavour component of herbs, spices, and fruits. Infusion extracts these compounds from the ingredient, which then dissolve in the alcohol.

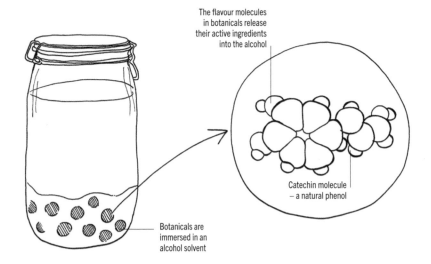

The flavour molecules in botanicals release their active ingredients into the alcohol

Botanicals are immersed in an alcohol solvent

Catechin molecule – a natural phenol

THE PRACTICE

Sloe Gin

For me, making sloe gin has gone from being a novice experiment to a yearly tradition I would never dream of missing. The berries are often easy to find, with minimal scratches for your efforts, and the drink is a perfect winter treat. Often the sloe berry season will overlap with blackberries, rosehips, or haw berries, and these all work well using the same process.

Figure a.

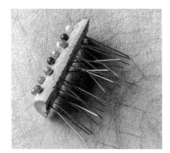

Figure b.

Figure c.

MAKES

1 litre (1¾ pints)

INGREDIENTS

450g (1lb) sloe berries
250g (9oz) caster sugar
750ml (1¼ pints) gin

EQUIPMENT

needle, skewer, or sloe pricker
2 x 1-litre (1¾-pint) wide-necked
    glass jars, sterilized
muslin or cheesecloth
1-litre (1¾-pint) glass bottle,
    sterilized
funnel

Method

01 Forage for the sloes in autumn, when they are still plump and juicy. I try to wait until after the first frost, but sometimes, if they've had a late summer of sunshine, you may need to pick them earlier.

02 Give the berries a good rinse under a cold tap, then prick their skins in several places so the flavoursome juice can leach out and the gin can get in **(fig. a)**. If you lack the patience to skewer each berry individually, freeze the sloes overnight to crack the skin once they thaw. Alternatively, use half a wine cork with two dozen needles pushed through it to create a multi-pronged sloe pricker **(fig. b)**. It's a superb tool for the job and saves a lot of time.

03 Put your pricked sloes into large glass jars, then add the sugar **(fig. c)** and gin. Firmly seal the lids and give the jars a really good shake.

04 Shake every day for the first few weeks to make sure that all the sugar dissolves and the sloes' flavour really infuses the gin. Thereafter I recommend rotating the sloe gin jars once every week or two.

05 Store out of direct sunlight for at least 1–2 months, if not 3, then strain the liquid through a sheet of muslin or cheesecloth into a bottle using a funnel. The leftover sugary sloes can be used for a fruity cider (see pp.88–89) or in a sauce with game. In my opinion sloe gin improves with age, so I tend to drink each batch a year later as a cheeky reward for my foraging efforts.

EXPERT TIPS

As a neutral white spirit, gin offers a blank canvas for flavour infusions; vodka and white rum would also work well.

—

I like intense flavoured spirits that can be detected in cocktails, so I tend to infuse for 2–3 months at least. However, you can leave infusions for 1–2 months for a subtler flavour. Taste regularly over the time period to find the strength you like best.

—

Forage considerately. Always try to leave a good percentage of berries on the branch so that wild birds like hawfinches can enjoy the seeds and thrushes or waxwings can eat the berry flesh.

THE POSSIBILITIES

A Spirited Guide

The fantastic thing about creating your own flavoured liqueurs is that they require very little specialist equipment and hardly any effort. The key is to select bold flavours that will work with your chosen alcoholic base.

COCKTAIL HOUR

Robust fruit, punchy spices, and foraged ingredients can transform your cocktail cabinet and open up more ideas to try in the kitchen.

- Try neat sloe gin as a starting point for a Prosecco top, a hot toddy with orange and clove, or a highball glass of lemonade or ginger ale with crushed ice.
- Bitters are made from different botanicals, from fruit to bark. Try infusing orange peel and juice in rum or brandy – this shrub is almost a cocktail in its own right but more intensely flavoured, so it works best as a cocktail mixer to add a sour, bitter note.
- My prediction is that craft vermouth will soon be as popular as craft gin. This fortified wine is flavoured with all sorts of botanicals, such as chilli, cloves, rosemary, star anise, and bay **(fig. a)**, and is a useful cocktail mixer.

———

Try ... Vermouth Have a play with 2 juniper berries, 1 teaspoon of dried orange peel, 2 cloves, 2 cardamom pods, 6 coriander seeds, 1 teaspoon of chamomile flowers, a pinch of fennel seeds, 1 bay leaf, 1 star anise, and 750ml

> *Blending botanicals is the closest a chef comes to truly understanding the magical world of the bartender. There is so much potential to add flavour, create balance, and pacify volatile ingredients.*

Figure a.

Figure b.

Figure c.

Figure d.

Figure e.

(1¼-pints) white or red wine. Put all the fruit and spices in a pan and cover with a quarter of the wine. Bring to a simmer and then heat on low for 10–15 minutes. Add 50g (1¾oz) caster sugar for a sweet vermouth (omit for dry vermouth), and allow to cool overnight in a sealed jar. Add 150ml (5fl oz) brandy, stir well, then strain through a lined sieve **(fig. b)** and combine with the remaining wine.

GO BOLD

You can create pretty much any flavour combination with spirits, from garlic vodka to ginger gin, as they can retain big flavours.

- Try seasonal fruits that pack a punch, including strawberries, oranges **(fig. c)**, lemons, cherries, and cranberries – use 250g (9oz) fruit per 1 litre (1¾ pints) spirit.
- Spices such as star anise, vanilla, clove, and lemongrass are all worth experimenting with.
- Make your own marmalade vodka to use in place of triple sec.
- Strong flavours such as chilli, garlic, or ginger can infuse quickly, in just 1–2 weeks.

Try ... Marmalade vodka (fig. d, left)
Start by adding the zest of 2 large oranges to a sterilized jar, then add the orange juice and 125g (4½oz) caster sugar, 1 cinnamon stick, and 1 star anise. Pour in 750ml (1¼ pints) vodka, seal the jar, and shake. Leave in a cool, dark place for 1 month, remembering to shake the jar every week, then strain and serve.

AROMATICS

If you want something a bit different that's subtle and sophisticated, give these aromatic botanical flavours a go.

- Start with oily herbs like rosemary and thyme, or aromatic flowers such as lavender and elderflower.
- Bourbon infused with smoked pears and a few sprigs of fresh thyme offers fruity depth and delicious caramel notes **(fig. d, right)**.
- Rose petals are wonderful added to gin; they give a slight pink tint and the resulting infusion makes for a superb twist on a classic G&T **(fig. e)**.

DAIRY

Project 11
YOGURT

Cultured milk transformed into a mildly tart, spoonable treat.

SKILL LEVEL Easy.

TIMINGS 6–12 hours for culturing and, depending on the type of yogurt, straining.

Ways with yogurt
Drink it, pour it, or spoon it – a pot of home-made yogurt is a joy to make.

THE SCIENCE

Cultured Milk

For thousands of years we have been enjoying forms of yogurt. There are some great stories surrounding its origins, from hot saddle bags of horse milk to wild bacteria fermenting milk in animal-skin pouches. Nowadays, all you need is milk, a starter, and clean equipment. The fermentation process cultures the milk, turning the sugars to lactic acid, causing it to thicken and sour, resulting in a tangy, luxurious delight.

FRIENDLY BACTERIA

Yogurt is created when bacterial cultures ferment warm soured milk to transform both the texture and the taste. The by-product of the fermentation process is lactic acid, which gives yogurt its signature sourness. Meanwhile the production of lactic acid reduces the pH level to below 5, causing the broken-down proteins to recombine and produce the creamy, gel-like texture of yogurt. The strains of friendly bacteria in yogurt normally include one or all of *Lactobacillus bulgaricus*, *Lactobacillus acidopholis* and *Streptococcus thermophilis*, and because these probiotic bacteria have already started to break down the milk, they make live yogurt easy to digest. At the same time they help to replenish healthy gut bacteria.

TEMPERATURE

The bacteria that ferment milk into yogurt are typically thermophilic bacteria, which means they become active at elevated temperatures. Therefore, to make nice, thick yogurt you must incubate it and maintain that warmth. Bacteria used in this process will survive at temperatures of 36–55°C (97–131°F), but these are the limits; either side of this range will kill your bacteria and cease the yogurt's development. The key range is 40–50°C (104–122°F), with ideal conditions at the upper limit of this. When within this optimum range, the bacteria feed on the milk's lactose sugars and start creating a new product within a few hours.

Gel formation
When milk ferments, the casein protein molecules link together to form a network of strands, trapping fat and water globules to make a gel.

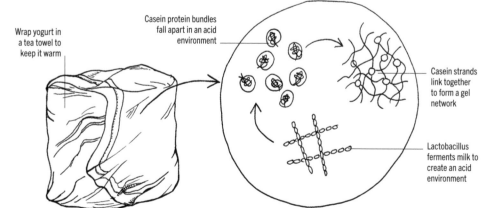

Wrap yogurt in a tea towel to keep it warm

Casein protein bundles fall apart in an acid environment

Casein strands link together to form a gel network

Thermophilic bacteria
The bacteria that create yogurt are activated by warmth, so the milk must be incubated.

Lactobacillus ferments milk to create an acid environment

THE PRACTICE

Raw Yogurt

Swaddling a pot of yogurt in tea towels and leaving it overnight in a warm corner of the kitchen has something almost parental about it. I especially love the excitement of returning in the morning to check for that delicate, quivering change as milk transforms almost magically into yogurt. You can of course sweeten it, but I love yogurt with a silky shudder of freshness and an acid snap.

Figure a.

Figure b.

Figure c.

MAKES

1 litre (1¾ pints)

INGREDIENTS

1 litre (1¾ pints) whole milk
75ml (2½fl oz) live yogurt,
    or 1g sachet of yogurt
    starter culture

EQUIPMENT

1-litre (1¾-pint) glass jar, sterilized

Method

01 Heat the milk slowly in a pan over a very low heat for 30 minutes until it reaches 46°C (115°F), stirring frequently so the milk doesn't catch on the bottom of the pan, then stir the live yogurt into the warm milk **(fig. a)**. Alternatively, if using a sachet culture, sprinkle in the starter and leave for 5 minutes to rehydrate.

02 Mix in the culture gently using a whisk, stirring with up and down motions. Next, you will need to maintain a constant temperature for the mixture of 40–50°C (104–122°F) for at least 4–6 hours. I heavily insulate the covered milk pan by wrapping it in towels, then leave it in a warm corner of the kitchen, which does the trick **(fig. b)**. You can even keep a hot-water bottle near it if needed. Alternatively, you can transfer the mixture to a sterilized glass jar or a yogurt-making machine (if you have one – see Expert Tips, right), seal with a lid, and keep at a constant temperature of 40–50°C (104–122°F) for 6 hours or overnight in a low oven, dehydrator, or on a shelf in an airing cupboard.

03 Once the yogurt thickens and develops a tangy quality, transfer it to a sterilized, sealable pot or glass jar **(fig. c)** and leave it in the fridge to set further. You should store yogurt at less than 4°C (39°F) and eat it within 10 days. You can also freeze it to make a delicious frozen yogurt.

EXPERT TIPS

Live yogurt is widely available and can be used as a starter culture. Commercial sachets of freeze-dried yogurt starter are available online and are a little more reliable, but if you eat yogurt regularly and want to save money, keep some reserved each time you make a batch.

Commercial yogurt-making machines are effective, convenient, and affordable, but they lack the cottage-charm of doing it manually. Their main advantage is that they are excellent at controlling and maintaining the correct temperature for the 6–8-hour culturing process.

You can heat the milk to at least 82°C (180°F) first, then cool it down before adding in your starter. This sours the milk ready for the bacteria to thrive and denatures the curd proteins so that they will unwind more easily. It also kills off any unwanted bacteria and cooks some of the whey proteins, resulting in a thicker yogurt than the raw version.

THE PRACTICE

Kefir

Anyone who enjoys the lactic tang of live yogurt will enjoy a cold glass of fresh kefir. It contains more beneficial bacteria strains than natural yogurt, making it not only better for our health, but also more resilient to lower fermentation temperatures, allowing it to continue to ferment even in the fridge. The sour taste and effervescent texture lift smoothies and marinades to the next level.

MAKES
___

1 litre (1¾ pints)

INGREDIENTS
___

1 litre (1¾ pints) whole milk
1 tsp kefir grains

EQUIPMENT
___

1.5-litre (2¾-pint) glass jar,
   sterilized
muslin or cheesecloth
sieve (plastic or stainless steel,
   not a reactive metal)
1-litre (1¾-pint) glass bottle,
   sterilized
funnel

Method

01 Warm your milk in a pan to 32°C (90°F), then stir in
your kefir grains. Pour into a glass jar, cover with a
square of muslin and secure with string or an elastic
band, then leave at room temperature for 12–24 hours
for the milk to sour and the kefir to develop its flavour.
I shake or stir the mixture every few hours to help the
milk ferment evenly throughout **(fig. a)**. Fermentation
will take less time if in a warm environment and more
if it's colder. The longer you leave it, the stronger the
taste will become.

02 After you've cultured your kefir, strain through a sieve,
transferring the kefir liquid to a glass bottle using a
funnel and retaining the kefir grains to make another
batch **(fig. b)**. Store the fermented kefir in the fridge
and consume within 7–10 days.

03 To restart the process, add another 1 litre (1¾ pints)
warm milk to your kefir grains **(fig. c)** and leave again
for 12–24 hours at room temperature.

EXPERT TIPS
___

You can purchase a kefir starter
powder online or buy milk kefir
grains. I prefer using grains, as they
grow over time and you can share
them with friends and family. They
also have more probiotics and,
with proper care, can be used
indefinitely, whereas powders
will eventually cease culturing.

_____

Rinse the kefir grains in between
batches in cold water and avoid
using any strong cleaning products
on the container, as they could
taint the fermentation.

_____

If you are going away, you can feed
your kefir mother and leave it in a
little milk in the fridge until you
return, when you can reactivate it
with more warmth and milk. Only
do this after 3–4 weeks of culturing
it regularly, though.

Figure a.

Figure b.

Figure c.

Different Cultures

Yogurt is so versatile; it can substitute for mayonnaise, be dolloped into soup or salad dressings, or be frozen as a dessert. Equally, it's the ultimate boost to your breakfast.

IT'S ALL GREEK TO ME

Greek yogurt is thicker and richer than plain yogurt, but the process is very similar. I make mine using half whole milk and half cream, but try ewe's milk for a more authentic taste.

- I love using home-made Greek yogurt infused with spices as a marinade for fish, lamb, and poultry.
- Make a light ranch dressing or cooling tzatziki dip with garlic, mint, and grated cucumber. Great for summer barbecues.

Try ... Greek yogurt Gently heat 500ml (16fl oz) whole milk and 500ml (16fl oz) double cream to bring it to 82°C (180°F) over the course of 1 hour, then submerge the base of the pan in a bowl of ice and whisk until the temperature drops to 38–40°C (100–104°F). Add 1 drop of rennet and 75ml (2½fl oz) live yogurt. Stir well for 2 minutes, then cover and leave for 6–8 hours at room temperature. The curds should form a solid mass, so stir with a rubber spatula to break them into chunks. Cover again and leave for 10–15 minutes. Drain

> "
> *You should never run out of yogurt; always try to reserve some to start off the next batch. I like to let this rolling-culture approach banish waste in the artisan kitchen.*
> "

Figure a.

Figure b.

Figure c.

the curds in a lined colander for 20 minutes
or until the whey stops dripping, then transfer
to a pot in the fridge and eat within 1 week.

THE BREAKFAST CLUB

For a bright breakfast built on glossy cultured
yogurt, add flavours and layered textures.

- For an enticing gourmet pot, add some more
  unusual treats such as granola, toasted nuts,
  and seeds, Turkish delight, and jams **(fig. a)**.
- A generous drizzle of yogurt can cut
  through rich or overly sweet breakfasts.
  It's particularly good with waffles, bacon,
  and maple and blueberry syrup.
- Try a ginger and turmeric lassi for an Indian
  take on a breakfast milkshake **(fig. b)**.

Try ... Ginger and turmeric lassi Blend
200ml (7fl oz) plain yogurt with 1 chopped
banana, 1 teaspoon of grated fresh root ginger,
and ½ teaspoon of turmeric. Add 1 teaspoon
of honey to sweeten, and slacken the lassi with
3 tablespoons of chilled whole milk.

THE THICK OF IT

Tangy, creamy, and extra-strained for added
thickness, labneh is basically yogurt cheese.

- Roll into balls and dust lightly with za'atar
  or dried mint and toasted cumin seeds for a

delicious appetizer. Serve with lychees, honey,
and lemon.

- Thicker labneh can be spread on toast and
  topped with cucumber shavings, dill, and
  caper berries.
- Serve with grilled flatbread in a bowl with
  a generous drizzle of olive oil, pomegranate
  seeds, mint, sumac, and fresh figs to garnish.

Try ... Labneh Stir 1 teaspoon of salt into
1 litre (1¾ pints) yogurt (either natural goat's
milk or quality full-fat cow's milk yogurt), then
pour into a jelly bag or several layers of muslin
with the edges tied, and hang, allowing it to
strain over a bowl for 6–12 hours **(fig. c)**. The
longer you leave the yogurt, the heavier the
labneh's texture will be. Store in a sealed
container in the fridge and use as a spread, like
cream cheese. It will keep for up to 2 weeks.

Project 12
BUTTER

A creamy, hand-churned dairy spread and cooking ingredient.

SKILL LEVEL Easy.

TIMINGS 12–24 hours
for ripening the cream;
1 hour for making the butter.

Hand-churned butter
The fat solids from
churned and separated
cream are moulded into
smooth pats of butter.

THE SCIENCE

De-emulsification

To make butter, soured cream is placed in a container, often a churn, and mixed and shaken to de-emulsify it until the fat separates from the liquid and comes together as butter. Traditionally people would do this as part of their domestic routine using milk and cream from the family cow. Now, you don't need a cow or even a sterile dairy to create delicious butter.

BUTTERFAT

Milk and cream are emulsions of fat globules suspended in water. The bigger the fat globules, the slower they move and the thicker the milk or cream becomes. Cream is far higher in fat content than milk, making it perfect for butter-making. To turn cream into butter you should sour it first by encouraging bacteria to turn some of the lactose – the sugar that makes cream naturally sweet – into lactic acid. Some butter is made from sweet fresh cream, but I prefer to make cultured butter from acidic soured cream. The acidification is achieved either by fermentation (by adding a live yogurt culture or kefir) or adding lemon juice to lower the pH, producing a rich butter with a fuller, slightly tangy flavour.

CHURNING AND SEPARATION

Churning is an extremely simple process that can be powered by a churn or a standard electric whisk. The method involves whipping or beating the cream until it looks like scrambled eggs and turns slightly yellow. This churning process agitates the cream until the membrane around the milk solids is broken, allowing the fat globules to clump together. As you keep churning, fat clusters surround air bubbles, which trap the liquid part of the cream; this is known as the "foam" stage. As the clumps get larger they can no longer surround the bubbles, which pop so that the solids and liquid separate. Once you separate off the buttermilk, you're left with the fat solids, which can then be moulded into a smooth butter.

Churning
As cream is churned, air is beaten into it and fat globules clump together to surround the air, creating a foam. Eventually the fat clumps become too large to enclose the air bubbles, causing the foam structure to collapse and the cream to separate into fat solids and buttermilk.

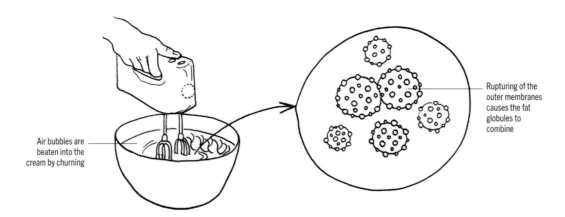

Air bubbles are beaten into the cream by churning

Rupturing of the outer membranes causes the fat globules to combine

THE PRACTICE

Salted Butter

Butter is a vital ingredient in so much cooking and is, in fact, extremely quick, easy, and fun to make. The key to fantastic butter is to churn your cream for long enough to get all the buttermilk out and then take your time washing and drying it properly. Remember to have fun shaping your butter and adding your personal maker's mark to the finished pat.

Figure a.

MAKES

4 x 250g (9oz) pats of butter

INGREDIENTS

2.5 litres (4 pints) double cream
2 tbsp live natural yogurt
2 tbsp fine sea salt

EQUIPMENT

electric whisk
sieve
muslin or cheesecloth
wooden butter bats or spatulas

Figure b.

Figure c.

Figure d.

Method

01 Pour the cream into a clean, sterilized bowl. Add the live yogurt and stir. Leave at room temperature for 6–12 hours for the cream to ripen.

02 Beat the ripened cream with an electric whisk for 4–5 minutes until it forms soft peaks **(fig. a)**. Keep going until the cream gets stiffer and eventually turns pale yellow in colour and looks more like scrambled eggs.

03 After 2–3 minutes more, small globules of butter will form, surrounded by milk foam bubbles. Add 1 tablespoon of cold, clean water when the mixture looks like a firm mass of butter globules, and carry on whisking for 1 minute on a low speed. Strain the butter through a sieve lined with muslin or cheesecloth, then pour off the buttermilk and retain for use in other recipes (see p.111).

04 Next, squeeze the butter on a wooden board and press dry with a cold sheet of muslin or cheesecloth **(fig. b)**. Rinse and ring out the cloth regularly until the water pressed from the butter runs clear rather than cloudy. Keep working until the butter is clean and dry.

05 Add the 2 tablespoons of salt to the butter (or at least 2 per cent of the butter's weight in salt), sprinkling a little at a time from a height for good coverage **(fig. c)**, then folding it in with your hands. This is primarily to preserve it for longer but will also add flavour. Fold the salt in thoroughly.

06 Divide the mixture into 4 and use grooved butter bats or wooden spatulas to press into blocks **(fig. d)** - the bats need to be cold and wet, so dip them in icy water first. Push down firmly to drive out any air bubbles.

07 Shape into 4 pats or rolls, or use moulds. Groove or stamp the surface to decorate and wrap in baking parchment. Alternatively, squash the butter into sterilized containers with lids. Butter can be frozen for up to 3 months and used straight from the freezer. If stored in the fridge, eat within 3 weeks.

EXPERT TIPS

I use double cream for butter for the highest fat content possible; over 40 per cent is ideal. If the cream is at the right temperature – about 20°C (68°F) – the butter will "come" (the term for when it changes from cream to butter) in a matter of minutes. Too cold and you will be churning for longer and the butter will be harder to work with.

If using a butter mould, ram the butter in hard to push out any air bubbles. If you buy or make your own butter stamp for decoration, remember to dip it in cold water before pressing to stop it sticking.

THE POSSIBILITIES

Butter Up

Going beyond basic salted butter to flavoured, cultured, or clarified versions allows you to incorporate more layers of flavour when you are cooking.

FLAVOURED BUTTER

Adding your own flavours to home-made butter provides a quick cheat when cooking.

- Stick to classic herbs and spices to begin with: roasted garlic and parsley; smoked salt or chilli; lime and coriander **(fig. a)**.
- Seaweed butter is superb with grilled white fish or when used to cook mussels before steaming. Also try with surf and turf – lobster and steak – for a decadent feast.
- Some combinations are truly special: anchovy butter with lamb; chimichurri butter with steak; truffle butter in mashed potato; bacon and cinnamon butter with French toast.

Try ... Seaweed butter Soften 100g (3½oz) butter for 1 hour. Beat with a wooden spoon until soft, then add 1 tablespoon of dried seaweed (see p.65). Tip the butter onto a square of baking parchment, roll into a sausage shape, and twist the ends to seal **(fig. b)**. Use within 7 days if refrigerated or 3 months if kept in the freezer.

CLARIFIED BUTTER

If you heat butter to encourage further separation, you can skim off the milk solids that float on the surface, leaving a clarified butter that will store for longer. Indian ghee is extra clarified – cooked for longer to remove even more solids.

Figure a.

Figure b.

Figure c.

Figure d.

- The remaining milk solids in ghee caramelize as it cooks before being strained out, lending it a nuttier flavour and darker colour **(fig. c)**.
- Spicing ghee with cumin, ginger, cardamom, fenugreek, or turmeric works extremely well.

BUTTERMILK

Buttermilk isn't just a by-product; it's a key ingredient in the kitchen in its own right.

- Buttermilk or whey sodas are tasty if you ferment them with kefir grains.
- Brining with buttermilk helps keep chicken and fish moist before frying and adds a lovely sour note to marinades.
- The Strawbridge family recipe for pancakes is the best use of buttermilk I can think of.

Try ... My granny's famous pancake recipe
Beat 1 large egg in a bowl, add 85g (3oz) caster sugar, then sift in 225g (8oz) soda flour blend (225g/8oz plain flour, ½ teaspoon of bicarbonate of soda, ½ teaspoon of cream of

> " *It's well known that most chefs love cooking with butter – it's one of the cornerstones of classic French cookery. I'm a believer that if you're generous with the quantity of butter in your recipes, you can't go far wrong.* "

tartar, ¼ teaspoon of salt) a little at a time. Gradually pour in 500ml (16fl oz) buttermilk while beating with a wooden spoon, then set aside. Heat a seasoned griddle pan so that it is warm but not too hot. Next, drop a ladleful of batter onto the griddle and wait for 1–2 minutes. Watch for the air bubbles rising to the surface, then flip and cook for 30 seconds on the other side. Stack under a tea towel until you are ready to serve with butter **(fig. d)**.

Project 13
CHEESE

Rich, firm, savoury dairy decadence.

SKILL LEVEL Difficult: the challenge is often the final maturing stages for pressed cheese.

TIMINGS Initial coagulation time 40–60 minutes, plus 1 hour for the cut curds to solidify further.

The artisan cheeseboard
Home-made goat's cheeses with sourdough crackers, fresh figs, grapes, and fig chutney.

THE SCIENCE

Curds and Whey

The science of cheese-making is fascinating. The proteins in cultured milk coagulate when you add rennet, then as heat is applied the milk separates into solid curds and liquid whey. It is the curds that are then salted, shaped, and matured to form cheese. The rich history of cheese-making may fill you with trepidation at the thought of making your own, but stay clean, organized, and follow the recipes, and there's nothing to fear.

COAGULATION AND SEPARATION

To make cheese, milk is warmed gradually so the proteins are activated but not destroyed, then a starter culture is added. The lactic acid bacteria in the starter culture convert the lactose sugars in the milk to lactic acid, giving it a sour, tart taste. Next, rennet is added, which is a complex group of enzymes that comes from the stomach of a calf, goat, or lamb and solidifies the casein proteins in milk, causing it to split and form solid curds (milk solids, fats, and proteins) and liquid whey (mostly water). The process of coagulation works in tandem with the growth of bacteria, while the correct temperature for the bacteria to thrive and the rennet to work (32–37°C/90–99°F) must be maintained. The curds and whey can then be separated.

PRESERVATION AND MATURATION

Once the curds have been pressed and shaped into cheese, salting and maturation are the final steps. Dry-salting the cheese's surface before or after shaping will dissolve the salt in the surface moisture and draw out the water from inside via osmosis. The water can then evaporate. This process not only adds flavour; it helps to form a dehydrated rind and protects the cheese from unwanted bacteria. The other option is to brine your shaped cheese in a solution of salt and sterilized water. This serves the same purpose but works more internally. Leaving cheese in a cool place to mature allows the enzymes and bacteria to continue to build flavour, alter proteins, and develop texture – and this can take anywhere from 2 weeks to several years.

Maturation
Mould and bacteria feed on the fats, sugars, and proteins in cheese, breaking them down into smaller molecules with distinct flavours.

Forming the rind
Cheese can be sprayed with a solution of edible mould spores to create a bloomy rind, or with a brine solution that contains ripening bacteria for a washed rind.

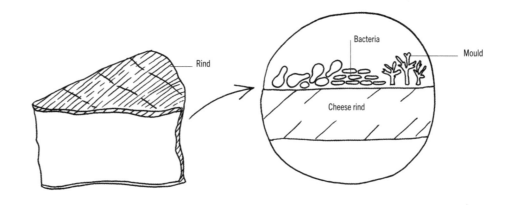

Rind

Bacteria

Mould

Cheese rind

MAKES

4 x 200g (7oz) blocks of feta-style
cheese

INGREDIENTS

5 litres (8¾ pints) goat's milk
500ml (16fl oz) buttermilk
6–8 drops of rennet, dissolved in
    1 tbsp sterilized water
4 tbsp sea salt flakes
1 litre (1¾ pints) medium-strength
    brine – 150g (5½ oz) salt per
    1 litre (1¾ pints) sterilized water

EQUIPMENT

thermometer
colander
cheesecloth
feta cheese mould (optional)
draining rack
sealed container for brining,
    sterilized

THE PRACTICE

My Feta-style Cheese

This is my twist on a renowned crumbly cheese that made an impression
on me when enjoying a holiday in Greece. It's a great starting point for
making your own cheese because you get to try out multiple techniques,
but the recipe is pretty forgiving for first-timers. Then, once you feel like
an accomplished maker of soft cheese, you can move on to the next level
to master more artisan skills.

Figure a.

Method

01 Heat your milk slowly in a pan for 20 minutes until it reaches 32°C (90°F) – check the temperature using a thermometer. Mix in the buttermilk and keep the pan at a constant temperature for an hour while the milk ripens. I use a water bath with a temperature of about 35°C (95°F) to hold the pan in, or a soup-kettle can be very effective, but other options include covering the pan with a lid and wrapping it with plenty of tea towels to insulate your milk.

02 Add the rennet and stir gently for a couple of minutes **(fig. a)**. Leave for 1 hour, maintaining the same temperature, while the curds and whey form. To test whether the curd is ready, insert a knife or your finger into the curd at a slight angle. The edge of the curd should break cleanly with a sharp rather than soft edge, and the gap should fill with whey. If the cut leaves your curds messy and soft-edged then leave for another 10–15 minutes. If you are happy with the test, cut the curds into 1cm (½in) cubes **(fig. b)** and leave to rest for 15 minutes, undisturbed, at a maintained temperature of 32°C (90°F).

03 Ladle the curd cubes out of your separated whey and into a colander lined with cheesecloth **(fig. c)**, then leave to drain for 1 hour.

04 Next, if you have one, transfer the curds to a cheese mould lined with cheesecloth and spread the curds out into the corners. Set this on a draining rack and leave for 4 hours. If you don't have a cheese mould, leave the curds in the lined colander for another 4 hours. Remove them from the mould or colander and flip every hour or so for a uniform-looking cheese.

05 Once drained, chop your cheese into 4 blocks and sprinkle evenly with 1 tablespoon of the sea salt flakes, then leave covered under an upturned bowl in the fridge for 2–3 days. Sprinkle with another tablespoon of salt every 24 hours, turning the cheese blocks over and pouring off any extra expelled whey.

06 If storing the cheese for any length of time, keep it refrigerated in a sealed container in a medium-strength brine solution. Once brined, this cheese should stay edible for 2–3 months. Alternatively, instead of curing with dry salt you could place the drained cubes straight into a light brine solution and consume within 2–3 weeks.

EXPERT TIPS

Use whole or semi-skimmed milk to make cheese (avoid skimmed milk). You can use homogenized milk, but you will get best results with unhomogenized or raw milk. Pasteurized milk is fine, as long as you use an effective starter and allow the lactic-acid bacteria to develop overnight before you begin.

———

If you don't have a cheese mould, make tiny holes in the sides and bottom of a plastic food container to allow the whey to escape.

———

Many recipes will ask you to apply weight to press cheese and expel any remaining whey. This is most easily done in a cheese-press but can be improvised with heavy bottles or tin cans.

Figure b.

Figure c.

The Big Cheese

With over 1,500 types of cheese in France alone, it's fair to say you can carve out your own niche if you want to create something distinct and different.

THE ALL-ROUNDER

Halloumi is ideal for cooking. It has a firm enough texture to treat like tofu or chicken and its salty, tangy taste is robust enough to pair with spices and other strong flavours.

- Slice, dust in seasoned flour, dip in egg and then panko breadcrumbs before deep-frying until golden for succulent halloumi fries.
- For a fantastic flavour combination, fry sliced halloumi, then add rose, sumac, and za'atar with pickled walnuts and fresh figs **(fig. a)**.
- Give a breakfast bap a facelift using halloumi instead of bacon with confit cherry tomatoes, samphire, coriander, and fermented red chilli.

Try ... Halloumi Heat 5 litres (8¾ pints) goat's milk to 25°C (77°F), add 10 drops of rennet, then remove from the heat and leave in a warm place to coagulate and separate for 1 hour. Test the curds with your finger and if they break cleanly, cut into 1cm (½in) pieces. Allow to rest for 5–10 minutes in the pan. Lift the curds carefully out of the whey and into a colander lined with cheesecloth. Sprinkle with salt and leave to drain for 15 minutes. Set aside the whey in the fridge, then press the curds into a tomme cheese mould and leave under a heavy weight for 3 hours. Heat the whey slowly for half an hour to 87°C (189°F), but don't allow it to boil. Cut the curds into smaller blocks and

Figure a.

Figure b.

Figure c.

Figure d.

Cheese-making is an artisan craft that takes complete kitchen commitment and a degree of romantic infatuation. You must fully focus and invest, in a way that borders on obsession.

add to the whey **(fig. b)**. Cook for 30–40 minutes or until the curds float, then skim out the cheese and air-dry for 1 hour, flipping occasionally. Store in a sterilized glass jar, either in whey in the fridge for 2–5 days, or in a medium brine solution for up to 2 months.

WAX ON

For Dutch-style Gouda, coat the finished cheese with different-coloured wax so you know which is which: traditionally red for plain, green for herby, orange for spiced **(fig. c)**.

- Grate into a macaroni cheese with truffle to elevate a humble comfort food.
- Try making a hearty pie with diced Gouda cheese, mixing it with spinach, roasted squash, fenugreek, and puy lentils.
- Dutch-style waxed cheese works particularly well when melted by an open fire for an alpine-style raclette.

UNDER PRESSURE

Curds packed tightly into a cheese mould and pressed with a 5kg (11lb) weight **(fig. d)** for 12 hours is often called Cheddar, after Cheddar Gorge, where it is aged in underground caves.

- Artisan Cheddar has a bold flavour that can stand up to sweet-spiced chutney, pickled onion, and fresh fruit. A ploughman's is still a great way to plate cheese with simplicity and allow its richness to shine.
- Grilled cheese on toast is one of the ultimate comfort foods. Toasted sourdough with thickly sliced Cheddar and umami-rich Worcestershire sauce, cooked until the cheese bubbles, is always a winner.
- For a more unusual pairing, try using a crumbly farmhouse pressed cheese baked with tart apples.

This is what working with dairy means to me: spending time on a process that's rustic while also being exact, requiring patience, attention to detail, and an almost clinical focus on cleanliness. The culture is intoxicating and holds a special place in the artisan's heart.

"

BREAD

Project 14
SOURDOUGH

Milk-sour aerated bread made with cultivated wild yeast.

SKILL LEVEL Medium:
keeping the starter lively
and kneading dough to
form strong threads of
gluten takes practice.

TIMINGS 7–10 days
prep; 12–24 hours for
proving and shaping.

Sourdough loaves
Richer, tangier, airier,
and healthier than
commercial bread.

THE SCIENCE

Wild Yeast Fermentation

The complex flavour of sourdough comes from the slow, symbiotic fermentation of the flour by wild yeasts and beneficial bacteria. Lactobacillus and other acid-producing bacteria in the starter produce lactic and acetic acids, which give the bread its sourness. The prebiotic content and the fermentation's breakdown of the gluten structure make it easier to digest than breads made with baker's yeast. The process may be slower than conventional baking, but it delivers a tastier bread and a distinctive texture.

STARTER CULTURE

A starter culture, or levain, is a mix of flour and water fermented by wild yeasts and lactic acid bacteria. Individually these components aren't that tasty, but the combination of by-products from the microbes' complex ecosystem produces the sweet-sour flavours and airy texture we love in this bread. The wild yeasts in sourdough are varied, rather than the one species in baker's yeast, and their coexistence makes each levain unique. As they convert the sugars in flour to carbon dioxide, the gas gets trapped in the dough as bubbles, which lift the bread as it bakes, creating a random honeycomb structure. Lactic acid bacteria are the dominant culture, but other bacteria and yeasts play their part, producing acids that attack unwanted microbes.

ACIDITY

The bacteria in sourdough produce lactic and acetic acids, and when this causes the bread's pH level to go below 4, the acidity breaks down the mineral bonds, making the nutrients easier for us to absorb. The benefit in terms of taste is that the lactic acid provides a rich flavour and the acetic acid supplies the zingy tang. Getting this flavour balance right can be tricky, but if your bread is too sour, you can make it less so by slowing the metabolic and reproductive rates of the lactobacilli. These microorganisms are more active at higher temperatures and when well hydrated, so reducing these factors will temper the sourness. This leaves yeast in the driving seat, resulting in a faster rise and less time for the bacteria to generate acids.

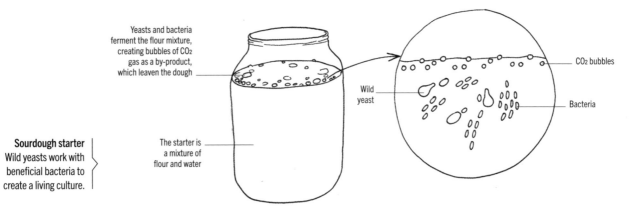

Yeasts and bacteria ferment the flour mixture, creating bubbles of CO_2 gas as a by-product, which leaven the dough

Sourdough starter
Wild yeasts work with beneficial bacteria to create a living culture.

The starter is a mixture of flour and water

Wild yeast

CO_2 bubbles

Bacteria

Sourdough Starter

My sourdough starter was appropriately named by my eldest son, Indiana, as "Bubbly Mummy". It's now a few years old and is treated with great respect as a family pet. Working with a living organism has as much to do with intuition as it does the recipe, so be attentive. Keep fermentation constant by feeding the starter regularly and maintaining the same hydration levels and temperature.

Figure a.

Figure b.

Figure c.

MAKES

1kg (2¼lb) starter

INGREDIENTS

500g (1lb 2oz) organic strong white
   bread flour
500g (1lb 2oz) water (see Expert
   Tips, right)

EQUIPMENT

1-litre (1¾-pint) glass jar, sterilized
muslin or cheesecloth

Method

01 Mix 400g (14oz) of the flour with 400g (14oz) of the
water in a glass jar **(fig. a)**. Whisk well and cover with
a piece of muslin or cheesecloth **(fig. b)**. Leave out of
harm's way at a constant temperature between 15 and
27°C (59–81°F).

02 After 1–2 weeks the starter will begin to ferment and
increase in volume. You will see bubbles start to form
and the consistency should be like a smooth, runny
porridge that falls off a spoon slowly but in a
continuous stream **(fig. c)**. Add the remaining flour
and water, and after 24 hours the starter will appear
lively, with a pleasant sour smell.

03 Once fully active, the starter will need frequent
attention to keep it alive. When stored at room
temperature feed daily with equal amounts of flour
and water – 2 tablespoons of each will suffice. If kept in
the fridge, however, the starter will only require feeding
twice weekly, with 2 tablespoons each of flour and
water. To avoid an increase in volume, remove 2–4
tablespoons of the starter mixture before feeding.

04 When you use some of the starter to make a loaf, you
will have to replace what you take away. For example,
if you use 150g (5½oz) starter in your recipe, replace it
with 75g (2½oz) flour and 75g (2½oz) water, whisked
into the original starter. With practice and careful
feeding, your starter can last for months if not years,
making loaf after loaf.

EXPERT TIPS

For exact quantities in bread-
making, I weigh liquids rather than
relying on volume measures. The
advantage is that scales are more
accurate than judging the level of
the liquid in a measuring jug by eye,
plus you can add everything into
one bowl on a set of scales.

———

Make a starter 2–3 weeks ahead of
when you plan to start baking. If
you are not baking every day, keep
your starter in the fridge and take it
out 24 hours before you need it, to
kick-start it into action. You can
also freeze it. To bring it back to life
again, let the liquid defrost and
leave it at room temperature for a
day before feeding it.

———

You can add some established
cultures when beginning a
sourdough starter to get it going.
Many people use a tablespoon of
natural yogurt in with the flour and
water to work alongside the wild
yeasts. I sometimes use milk kefir
as a direct stand-in for my
sourdough starter.

MAKES

1 sourdough loaf

INGREDIENTS

150g (5½oz) active sourdough
    starter (see pp.124–25)
250g (9oz) warm water
25g (scant 1oz) olive oil
500g (1lb 2oz) organic strong
    white bread flour
10g (¼oz) fine sea salt
50g (1¾oz) sprouted seeds – I use
    a mix of green and brown lentils,
    adzuki beans, sunflower seeds,
    mung beans, and chickpeas
    (optional)
2 tbsp linseeds or milled bran
    flakes

EQUIPMENT

dough scraper (optional)
bread lame, razor, or serrated knife
banneton (proving basket)

THE PRACTICE

Seeded Sourdough

A classic sourdough is always a winner, but if you want to add a lighter,
sunnier layer to your loaf then knead some sprouted seeds into the
dough. They remain a little crunchy after baking but are easy to digest
and offer a fresh complement to the sour tang. This is the ideal way to
get even more nutrition and flavour into your daily loaf.

Figure a.

Method

01 Whisk the starter, water, and olive oil in a large bowl. Add the flour and salt, then squish everything together with your hands **(fig. a)** or a dough scraper until all of the flour is absorbed. Knead on a floured surface for 10–15 minutes until smooth and springy.

02 Form the dough into a rough ball and transfer to a bowl. Cover and leave to prove at 20–27°C (68–81°F) for a fast rise or overnight at 15–20°C (59–68°F). Do not allow the temperature to fall below 9°C (48°F) or fermentation will cease. Your dough is ready when it no longer looks dense and has almost doubled in size. This can take anywhere from 6 to 12 hours, depending on temperature and the potency of your starter.

03 Turn out the dough onto a floured surface, flatten, and then, starting at the top, fold the edge towards the centre **(fig. b)**. Give the dough a slight turn, then fold over the next section. Repeat until you have come full circle. Incorporate your sprouted seeds at this stage if using, working them into the dough until evenly distributed. Flip the dough and place it seam-side down, then gently cup the sides and rotate it with a gentle downward pressure. Repeat this process until the dough is smooth in shape and appearance **(fig. c)**.

04 Add the linseeds or milled bran flakes to the bottom of a floured banneton so that they stick to the loaf as it proves. Place the dough in the banneton, cover, and leave for a second, shorter rise of about 1–2 hours at 20–27°C (68–81°F), until the dough is a little puffy.

05 Preheat the oven to 200°C (400°F/Gas 6). Just before your bread goes into the oven, use a bread lame, razor, or serrated knife to make a few shallow slashes, about 10cm (4in) long, in the surface of the dough **(fig. d)**.

06 Bake for 40 minutes. During the last 10 minutes, crack open the oven door momentarily. This allows moisture to escape, leaving your bread with a crisp crust.

EXPERT TIPS

Scoring or slashing the top of your dough quickly before it bakes controls the final shape of the loaf, preventing the crust from tearing or popping in odd places. It's also a baker's signature, so be experimental and have fun coming up with your own unique patterns.

———

Try using 100 per cent rye flour for a second mother culture. Once you have mastered the white flour recipe, it's nice to experiment with a second sourdough starter that has a nuttier flavour.

Figure b.

Figure c.

Figure d.

THE PRACTICE

Focaccia

A sourdough starter gives focaccia a stronger structure and more flavour than baker's yeast. Experiment with different herbs and spices for topping your focaccia. Za'atar, capers, olives, pumpkin seeds, or thinly sliced potatoes and onions all work well and can elevate the taste. You can also include seasonal pesto into the bread to marble the dough with herbs.

Figure a.

Figure b.

Figure c.

MAKES

1 focaccia loaf

INGREDIENTS

100g (3½oz) sourdough starter
(see pp.124–25)
10g (¼oz) sea salt flakes, plus
1 tsp for sprinkling
400g (14oz) water
500g (1lb 2oz) strong white bread
flour
3 tbsp extra-virgin olive oil
3–4 sprigs of rosemary, leaves
stripped from the stems

EQUIPMENT

dough scraper (optional)

Method

01 Mix the starter, salt, and water in a bowl with the flour using your hands or a dough scraper **(fig. a)**. Knead on a floured surface for 15–20 minutes until smooth and silky **(fig. b)**, then form into a rough ball and place in a bowl. Drizzle with 1 tablespoon of the olive oil, cover, and set aside. Leave to rise at 20–27°C (68–81°F) for 6–12 hours until the dough has doubled in size.

02 Turn out the dough into a lined baking tray with deep sides. Ensure the baking parchment is oiled with another tablespoon of olive oil and knock back the sourdough gently so that it fills the tray. Leave covered for a further 1–2 hours to prove for a second time at 20–27°C (68–81°F).

03 Use your fingertips to gently knock back the dough one last time, making shallow indentations. Leave to prove for a final 45 minutes at 20–27°C (68–81°F).

04 Push the sprigs of rosemary into the indentations and sprinkle over 1 teaspoon of sea salt flakes **(fig. c)**.

05 Bake at 200°C (400°F/Gas 6) for 25 minutes until golden brown. Remove from the oven and transfer to a wire rack. While the focaccia is still warm, brush with the remaining olive oil, then leave to cool completely before serving.

EXPERT TIPS

Establish whether your dough is sufficiently kneaded using the window-pane test. After kneading for 15 minutes or so, hold the dough up to the light from a window and stretch it. A thin, opaque membrane should be visible, which indicates fully developed gluten. If the dough tears and breaks apart, keep kneading and try again after another 5 minutes.

———

Try using flour blends for focaccia, incorporating about 25 per cent farro, kamut, and enkir flour. All slightly lower in gluten but high in protein, these ancient grains add a nutty flavour to focaccia.

———

Due to the high hydration levels of this bread and the amount of oil used, focaccia can be a sticky dough to work with. If you are baking focaccia in a pizza oven, dust semolina flour onto the peel so that the dough doesn't stick.

Artisan Baker

There's a bread to suit any mood. The variety is almost overwhelming, but my advice is to start with what you love to eat, and then explore traditions from around the world.

A POCKETFUL OF RYE
———————

Pumpernickel is a dense, dark, highly textured traditional German bread **(fig. a)** slowly suffused with the sweetness of rye berries.

- It's tough to beat rollmops and cured fish or smoked mackerel pâté on pumpernickel.
- Try Danish *smørrebrød* toppings, such as cold cuts of meat and sliced gravlax with dill-pickled cucumber or smoked cheese.
- Pumpernickel with hot smoked sausages and a very generous serving of sauerkraut captures every taste on the palate.

Figure a.

Try ... Pumpernickel Start the day before baking. Mix 300g (10oz) rye flour, 300g (10oz) warm water and 50g (1¾oz) sourdough starter in a bowl. Then leave covered in a warm place to ferment for 12–14 hours. Next, combine 200g (7oz) rye berries (available from health-food shops or online), 200g (7oz) sliced rye bread, and 450g (1lb) warm water. Submerge the floating bits every so often and stir. The next morning, strain the liquid and discard the bread and berries. Heat 300g (10oz) of the soaker liquid in a saucepan until warm, then mix with the starter and an extra 250g (9oz) rye flour, 250g (9oz) rye flakes, 50g (1¾oz) molasses and 20g (¾oz) salt. Mix using your hands, then scoop into an oiled casserole dish or bread tin. Leave to rise for a few hours, covered, at 20–25°C (68–77°F). Place in a preheated oven at 200°C (400°F/Gas 6), with a cupful of water in a baking tray underneath to steam the bread and form a crust. Bake for 1 hour, then reduce the temperature to 180°C (350°F/Gas 4) and bake for another hour. Reduce again to 150°C (300°F/Gas 2) and bake for a final 3–4 hours, then turn off the oven and leave the bread to cool inside.

ENGLISH BREAKFAST
———————

Muffins have to be a serious contender for the quintessentially English bread. They are versatile and you can cook them in 10 minutes on a griddle or in a heavy-based frying pan.

Figure b.

Figure c.

> *Once you have dough at your fingertips, the world is your bakery. You can make a humble loaf in a tin, shape rustic baguettes or ciabatta, or use moulds for English muffins.*

- I'm an absolute sucker for classic eggs Benedict with ham and hollandaise, or eggs Florentine with spinach or kale.
- For a twist on the classics, try serving muffins with smoked salmon, seaweed hollandaise, samphire, and a poached egg **(fig. b)**.
- Muffins are fantastic served with maple bacon as a replacement for waffles with a blueberry syrup.

BUBBLY BRUNCH

The bubbly surface of crumpets (and their thinner alternative, pikelets) forms a perfect base for butter melting in golden rivulets, but can also make a decadent brunch alternative.

- For my rarebit version, toast some pikelets, then add flakes of smoked haddock and rich cheese rarebit sauce before grilling **(fig. c)**.
- Crumpets soak up flavour so try topping with poached egg, asparagus, and truffle.

MIX IT UP

Ask your local artisan baker questions and experiment with ancient grains, shaping, seasonal ingredients, and exciting toppings.

- Experiment with different flours: rye flour makes a dark, heavy bread with a slightly sour taste and chewy texture. Barley flour

makes a lovely, sweet-tasting sourdough and is extra delicious if you toast the flour first. Spelt is especially high in protein, vitamins, and minerals and naturally low in gluten.

- Add chia or linseeds to dough for texture and flavour, or try milling your own flour with ancient grains **(fig. d)**. Amaranth, quinoa, teff, buckwheat, spelt, and millet tend to be nuttier and easier to digest than modern cereals.
- Seasonal and foraged ingredients make a super addition to bread dough or a colourful topping. Try making a wild garlic and nettle pesto for focaccia, adding beetroot and grated horseradish for a vibrant pink dough, or incorporating the seeds from flower heads such as fennel and sunflowers for texture.

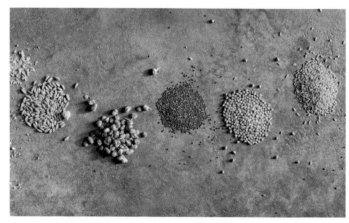

Figure d.

"

Baking is the beating heart of a kitchen. The simple pleasure of watching the magic of fermentation in action; feeling the change under your fingers as you knead; being rewarded with the comforting blast of sweet-sour bread emerging from a hot oven – it's unbeatable.

"

Project 15
FLATBREADS

Thin, tasty, tangy breads perfect for sharing.

SKILL LEVEL Easy: this is a quick and easy type of bread, ideal to make fresh.

TIMINGS 30 minutes prep; 1–2 hours fermenting; 10 minutes baking.

Chapatis
Flatbreads generally have a low volume and a large surface area.

THE SCIENCE

Fermented Flatbreads

When we trace the history of bread around the world, flatbreads are among the first examples, and as they are easy to make and taste delicious, their popularity has endured. Made with flour, water, and salt, they can be unleavened or leavened, but generally yeasts and raising agents are left out in favour of natural fermentation, resulting in a bread that is flat even when baked. Popular types include pizza, wraps, tacos, chapatis, and naans.

LEAVENED OR UNLEAVENED?

Leavened flatbreads such as naan or pitta undergo the same fermentation process as sourdough loaves, but the yeasts aren't given as much time to develop, making the breads flat, though still distinctively tangy in flavour. The wild yeasts and lactobacilli bacteria introduced by live yogurt or a sourdough starter will feed off the sugars in the flour and produce carbon dioxide, which aerates the dough with bubbles, creating a lighter-textured bread. The dough is often then knocked back and cooked quickly at high temperatures, so the yeasts don't have long to ferment. Unleavened breads like tortilla or matzah, which contain no added raising agents, will not rise in the same way, but often the laminated layers of fat in these breads – which sandwich steam that expands when baked, lifting apart the layers – can result in a pastry-like texture with decent volume.

MOISTURE CONTROL

Flatbreads generally have a large surface area, which means that as they cool steam can escape very quickly, leaving the bread dry and even brittle. A higher-protein flour such as durum wheat absorbs more water than a lower-protein soft grain like plain flour, so moisture levels may vary depending on the ingredients you use. This will directly affect the pliability of your flatbread but can be controlled according to personal preference. A flatbread can be baked dry into Scandinavian-style crispbreads or, like naan, retain moisture levels of over 35 per cent.

The flatbread "pocket"
When the dough is baked at a high temperature, steam is trapped between the layers, creating an air pocket.

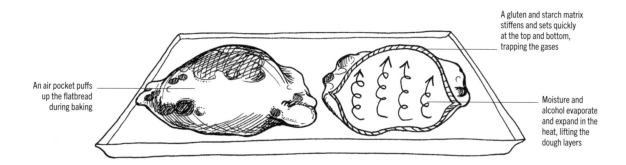

A gluten and starch matrix stiffens and sets quickly at the top and bottom, trapping the gases

An air pocket puffs up the flatbread during baking

Moisture and alcohol evaporate and expand in the heat, lifting the dough layers

THE PRACTICE

Naan

To me, a good naan bread is not just for mopping up a curry; it adds wonderful flavour and texture in its own right. By using a sourdough starter, you can make a flatbread with a slight sour tang that enlivens the taste buds and also provides the acidity to cut through a rich sauce. This naan has a crisp exterior and a soft, fluffy core – the perfect companion for your favourite curry.

MAKES

4 naan

INGREDIENTS

100g (3½oz) sourdough starter
    (see pp.124–27)
125g (4½oz) natural yogurt or
    milk kefir
350g (12oz) organic strong
    white bread flour
50g (1¾oz) warm water
1 tsp salt
50g (1¾oz) melted butter or ghee

Method

01 Mix all the ingredients except the melted butter or ghee in a large bowl **(fig. a)** until you get a rich, sticky dough. Cover and leave to rest at 21–25°C (70–77°F) for 30 minutes–1 hour to allow the gluten strands to develop and improve the texture of the dough, then knead on a floured surface for 15 minutes.

02 Shape into a rough ball, then cover and leave to prove for 4–6 hours at 21–25°C (70–77°F). The dough will rise only slightly during this period.

03 Once risen, knock back the dough, knead again gently, and divide into 4 pieces **(fig. b)**.

04 Roll out each piece on a floured surface and stretch until they are 5mm (¼in) thick. Leave on a baking tray lined with baking parchment for 45 minutes to prove for a second time (again, they will rise just a little).

05 Preheat the oven to 200°C (400°F/Gas 6). Brush each naan with a little melted butter or ghee for a rich gloss **(fig. c)** and bake for 10–15 minutes. Alternatively, cook on the hob in a hot cast-iron skillet or non-stick frying pan, for 4–5 minutes on each side, depending on the thickness of the naan. Flip when they start to bubble, and cook until browned and no doughy parts remain.

06 Whether using the oven or the hob, brush with more melted butter halfway through cooking. Serve warm.

EXPERT TIPS

To keep flatbreads more pliable after baking, wrap in a tea towel as soon as they are cooked. If you are making them in advance, reheat in the oven wrapped in foil, or fry in a little oil. Another option is to mist them with water before reheating.

———

A test for a very thin flatbread is to blow under it. If you want a really thin tortilla, for example, position it so that its edge overlaps the side of a chopping board, then bend down and blow towards the thin side. If it flutters like a handkerchief, it's plenty thin enough.

———

Traditionally flatbreads are baked in red-hot clay ovens or tandoors, but a baking stone will achieve a similar result. Baking stones are made from ceramics, stone, or salt and are heated before cooking. The thermal mass reduces the chance of burning the bread but provides a good, crisp base.

Figure a.

Figure b.

Figure c.

THE PRACTICE

Dosa

I learnt how to make traditional dosa when I was working with a lovely chef from Kerala. There was such grace in the way she made them. The swiftness of the smooth pour and the circular spreading of the batter was hypnotizing. She made it look easy, and after a batch or two you'll start to get the hang of it, too – as with crêpes, the first few might look rubbish but then you'll find your flow. If your batter is runny enough, you can make a lovely thin dosa, perfect as a tasty wrap for saag paneer, coriander, and chilli fried eggs, or spiced prawns.

Figure a.

Figure b.

Figure c.

MAKES

6 dosa

INGREDIENTS

100g (3½oz) sprouted seeds
500g (1lb 2oz) water
250g (9oz) rice flour
100g (3½oz) gram flour
50g (1¾oz) fresh spinach
15g (½oz) live yogurt
10g (¼oz) salt
1 tsp ground fenugreek
1 tsp ground cumin
½ tsp turmeric
1 tbsp chopped fresh coriander
1 tbsp melted ghee, for greasing

EQUIPMENT

food processor
non-stick frying pan or flat griddle
   (see Expert Tips, right)

Method

01   Blitz your sprouted seeds **(fig. a)** and all the other ingredients except for the melted ghee in a food processor until smooth. The texture of the batter should be like runny yogurt; it should fall off a whisk easily in a slow, continuous stream.

02   Once the batter is smooth, pour into a bowl, cover, and leave to ferment overnight at warm room temperature, about 15–25°C (59–77°F).

03   In the morning, the batter should have increased in volume and started to bubble **(fig. b)**. Whisk the batter again, then preheat a non-stick frying pan or flat griddle. Grease the pan with some melted ghee using a piece of kitchen paper so that it's evenly coated, then gently spread 1 large ladleful of the dosa batter into a round on the pan **(fig. c)**.

04   Drizzle a little ghee around the edge of the dosa and cook for 30 seconds–1 minute until browned, then flip and cook the other side for a few seconds.

05   Repeat the process for each dosa. Fold the cooked dosas or roll them up like a wrap and serve with an aromatic filling of your choice. Any leftover batter can be refrigerated and used within 4–5 days.

EXPERT TIPS

The sprouted seeds in this recipe can be substituted by sprouted or cooked urad dal (black lentils), which has the uncanny ability to help absorb wild yeasts and aid fermentation.

———

Buckwheat flour makes a delicious dosa batter and is easy to find. For a truly authentic idli dosa recipe, visit an Indian grocery store or shop online for black gram and idli rice.

———

A griddle is a cast-iron pan that can be heated to very high temperatures and can cook bread in seconds with little or no fat required. There are grooved varieties, which can add a lovely chargrilled stripe to your breads, though I prefer a smooth surface, as it's easier to clean and season. To test the temperature, drop a little water on the surface – the droplets should instantly sizzle and move around. If they evaporate on impact, the surface is too hot.

Fun with Flatbreads

Flatbreads have great flexibility – experiment with different flours and flavoured dough, stuff them with spices, or use them as wraps for stews and curries.

AFRICAN STAPLE

Injera is the Ethiopian national dish. It's a spongy, sour, slow-fermented flatbread made from teff flour and is perfect for sharing.

- Injera is generally served as a large, flat pancake with a selection of exotic curries (**fig. a**), collard greens, and stews such as the slow-cooked chicken dish doro wat. Try making a beef stew with berbere spice mix for another authentic topping.
- For a crispbread version that's great broken into shards and dipped into spiced lentils, salsa, or spiced cheese curds, bake at 180°C (350°F/Gas 4) for 1 hour with a drizzle of oil between 2 sheets of baking parchment.

Try ... Injera Combine 250g (9oz) teff flour, 250g (9oz) plain white flour, and 1 teaspoon of salt with 1kg (2¼lb) water. Mix well, then cover and leave for 12 hours. Stir and leave covered for a further 12 hours. Repeat for 3–4 days until the batter smells sour and bubbles. Next, heat a large, lightly oiled frying pan or flat griddle over a medium heat and pour in 2 ladlefuls of batter until a thin layer covers the pan. Cook for 10 minutes or until bubbles form on the surface. Do not flip. Remove from the heat and serve with dishes of your choice.

Figure a.

Figure b.

Figure c.

Figure d.

TASTY TORTILLAS

The greatest flatbread for rolling into a handy wrap has to be the humble tortilla.

- Cornmeal tortillas are thick and dense – perfect cut into segments and fried into crispy tortilla chips.
- The wheat flour tortilla makes a pliable wrap tasty to eat straight off the griddle. Use them as tacos filled with sizzling chicken or with pulled pork and pickles **(fig. b)**.

Try ... Tacos Combine 250g (9oz) white flour in a mixing bowl with 150g (5½oz) water, 1 teaspoon of salt, and a pinch of baking powder. Knead the dough for 10 minutes until elastic. Cover and leave in a ball to rest for 30–40 minutes at room temperature, then divide into equal-sized balls. Roll out on a floured surface until round and approximately 2mm (⅛in) thick. Place straight onto a dry, preheated griddle and cook for 30 seconds on each side.

FLAVOURED FLATBREADS

I first learnt how to make flatbreads in Nepal with a local tea-shop owner. My favourites were packed with fresh ingredients and big flavours.

- Treat flatbreads as a blank canvas. Enrich the dough with grated cheese or mashed root veg, or colour it using carrot or beetroot juice.
- Chapatis **(fig. c)** are excellent for mopping up dhal or a spicy chutney. Try adding chopped

> *Flatbreads are like a universal handshake. You can instantly have something in common with another artisan baker, wherever you come from.*

chilli and toasted cumin seeds to the dough.
- Fry a roti in hot oil with beaten egg for a twist on eggy bread. Serve with spicy chutney, lime zest, coriander, and red chilli.
- Embellish by sprinkling coconut, raisins, and flaked almonds over the top while cooking. Alternatively, a flatbread brushed with harissa butter, then sprinkled with garlic slices and dried rose petals, goes extremely well served with lamb koftas **(fig. d)**.

POTTING

——

Project 16
CONFIT

Slow-cooking in oil or fat for a rich, succulent consistency.

SKILL LEVEL Easy: a relatively straightforward artisan method that can achieve fantastic results.

TIMINGS 6–12 hours for curing; 4–8 hours for the confit; 2–3 months for preserving.

Confit cod
Slow-cooked in aromatic oil for a tender, moist texture and a rich flavour.

THE SCIENCE

Low and Slow

The term confit is used to describe just about anything that's cooked slowly – it can refer to poaching food in syrups, alcohols, or sugar, but the general sense for me is to immerse meat or fish in oil or fat, then heat it gently. Cooking times are measured in hours rather than minutes and cooking temperatures are kept low, which together preserve, tenderize, and boost the flavour of the produce by preventing moisture loss.

PRESERVATION AND FLAVOUR

The traditional confit method is to dry-salt meat and fish first, often with herbs and spices, in order to draw out moisture via osmosis – this deprives microbes of water, thus aiding preservation. Adding more salt afterwards further reduces any risk of botulism. Nowadays, however, confit is more about the intensified flavours that result from the immersion of the produce and the process of slow-cooking. For example, as with a marinade, confit meat is infused with flavour from the aromatics in the fat over time, but with the addition of heat this process becomes more volatile. The kinetic energy produced by heat causes the meat fibres to vibrate, encouraging the flavour compounds from the aromatics to impregnate the flesh.

TEXTURE

Confit cooking is done at a low temperature of around 90°C (194°F), which is key to breaking down the connective tissues in meat and fish and minimizing the loss of fluids. The tendons and ligaments in meat, for example, contain large amounts of collagen, which is tough to eat, but collagen starts to denature and break down at around 60°C (140°F), and at around 70°C (158°F) it dissolves into a rich liquid: gelatine. The low temperature, however, means that juices expelled from the muscle fibres during this process don't evaporate; they remain in liquid form, bound to the proteins within the meat. Immersing the produce in fat, which forms a hydrophobic barrier, also stops liquid escaping, resulting in a moist, succulent texture.

Collagen breakdown
Collagen is a tough protein found in ligaments and tendons, which at 60°C (140°F) starts to break down and dissolve into rich liquid gelatine.

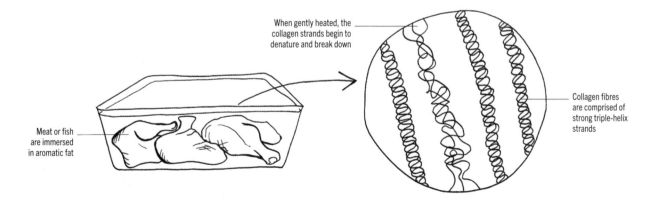

When gently heated, the collagen strands begin to denature and break down

Meat or fish are immersed in aromatic fat

Collagen fibres are comprised of strong triple-helix strands

THE PRACTICE

Confit Duck Legs

Confit duck is probably the most silky and succulent meat dish you can cook at home. I love finishing it simply in a pan to crisp the skin or shredding the meat and combining it with chestnuts and orange zest, then wrapping the mixture in a kale leaf. The flavourful fat can be used to sauté vegetables or cook potatoes, or makes a tasty addition to shortcrust pastry for pies and tarts.

Figure a.

Figure b.

Figure c.

MAKES

750g (1lb 10oz)

INGREDIENTS

4 x 220g (8oz) duck legs
1 litre (1¾ pints) olive oil, or
    duck or goose fat
For the cure
100g (3½oz) sea salt
50g (1¾oz) brown sugar
6 garlic cloves, crushed
4 star anise
1 tbsp pink peppercorns
1 cinnamon stick
1 tbsp grated orange zest
4 sprigs of thyme

EQUIPMENT

skewer
ovenproof casserole dish
2 x 1-litre (1¾-pint) glass jars,
    sterilized

Method

01   Use a skewer to pierce the duck skin and flesh several times so that the cure aromatics can penetrate **(fig. a)**.

02   Next, combine all the cure ingredients in a large casserole dish **(fig. b)** and toss the duck legs in the mixture. Really push the cure mixture into the pierced surface, then pack the legs tightly together in the dish. Scatter any remaining cure over the duck legs before covering and refrigerating for 6–12 hours. Turn the duck halfway through and pour away any liquid.

03   After curing, pat the duck dry with kitchen paper and brush off any cure. Keep some of the spices, garlic, and herbs to add to the confit later.

04   Place the duck in a large casserole dish and cover with the oil or fat, mixing in the reserved aromatics. Then cut out a cartouche (a piece of baking parchment large enough to cover the entire surface of the dish) and place over the duck. Weigh the duck down so that it sits below the fat using a small upturned ovenproof dish.

05   Slow-cook in the oven at 80°C (176°F) for 6–8 hours. You'll know it's ready when the meat comes away easily from the bone **(fig. c)**.

06   Transfer the confit meat to glass jars and seal with a layer of the cooking fat. This can be stored at low temperatures of under 4°C (39°F) for several months. Once opened, eat within 1 week.

EXPERT TIPS

Do not cook confit at temperatures above 90°C (194°F) – the water can start to evaporate from the produce and you will lose all that wonderful moistness.

———

Fish contains much lower collagen levels than meat (except for squid and octopus), so it will need a longer confit time.

———

Vegetables are quick to confit. Don't be afraid that they might turn out greasy; they will take on the spicy, nutty notes of a good oil, and in turn the oil will be infused with the sweetness or spiciness that the vegetables have to offer.

THE POSSIBILITIES

Confident Confit

There is very little that you can't cook confit – that's part of its magic. Plus, the sheer simplicity of it makes it such fun. This is a tradition that will never go out of fashion.

FAT IS FLAVOUR

Confit meat is particularly tender and succulent, as there's virtually no moisture loss.

- Confit chicken wings are remarkably juicy. Try glazing them in a spiced butter or coat in seasoned flour and deep-fry to finish.
- For amazing confit pork belly, brine the meat first, cook for 5–6 hours at 90°C (194°F), then deep-fry to crisp it up. Equally, confit carnitas is top notch – Mexican-style confit pork shoulder, shredded and served in a taco.
- Offal such as tongue, gizzards, and hearts confits well. Try serving confit duck hearts with a rose and quince jelly glaze.

CONFIT SECRETS

The most surprising ingredients can make a quick, successful confit. Textures become ultra-tender and flavours bold and intense.

- Confit garlic adds untold sweetness and umami depth to dishes. Smash and serve with green beans or peas, spread on crostini, or add to a broad-bean hummus.
- Try cherry tomatoes and red peppers with oregano and garlic cloves. Store in oil and use for quick pasta sauces or with grilled fish.
- Pea, mint, and bulgur wheat risotto works well with a confit egg yolk **(fig. a)** as a rich topping instead of Parmesan shavings.

Figure a.

Figure b.

Figure c.

Try ... Confit garlic Peel 2 bulbs of garlic **(fig. b)**. Place the cloves in a small saucepan and pour over enough olive oil to cover them. Bring to the boil, then reduce the heat to a minimum. Cook for 45 minutes–1hour until the garlic is soft and tender. Cool to room temperature and store in a sterilized jar in the fridge for 6–8 weeks. Try adding a sprig of rosemary or thyme to the oil along with the garlic as a variation.

FLAKY FISH

Confit is one method that's helped me to cook fish confidently. It's a superb way to keep fish moist and avoid overcooking it.

- A slow-cooked fillet of cod is fantastic and so easy; the oil accentuates the tender texture of the fish and enhances the richness of flavour.
- Adding a few garlic cloves, fennel seeds, or slices of lemon to your confit oil makes a huge difference to the taste of the fish.

Try ... Confit cod (fig. c) Cure two 150g (5½oz) cod fillets with 50g (1¾oz) sea salt. Leave for 30 minutes, then rinse in cold water and pat dry. Preheat the oven to 75°C (167°F). Place the cod in an ovenproof dish, adding slices of lemon, 1 teaspoon of fennel seeds, 1 tablespoon of capers, and 75g (2½oz) artichoke hearts. Heat 1 litre (1¾ pints) olive oil in a pan to 90°C (194°F) and pour over the fish. Cover with a cartouche and transfer to the oven. Bake for 15–20 minutes until the fish is opaque and has reached flaky perfection.

"

The French confit handbook has been passed down for hundreds of years. Throw it out of the window once you understand the principles – have fun and experiment.

"

Project 17
POTTING

Spreadable delights preserved under a rich layer of fat.

SKILL LEVEL Easy: just
keep your equipment clean.

TIMINGS 30 minutes–
12 hours curing; 2 hours
setting; 4–6 weeks storage.

Potted confit duck
Potting is a safe, simple
technique for preserving
pre-cooked produce.

THE SCIENCE

Barrier Preservation

Potted preserves like pâté, confit, or rillettes go in and out of fashion, but in the artisan kitchen they are an enduring favourite and a vital way to avoid waste. Potting is the simplest way to stop airborne organisms from spoiling food. Meat, fish, and vegetables are protected from oxidation under a thick barrier of fat – which also happens to be extremely tasty.

FAT BARRIER

Creating a thick layer of fat, which forms an airtight seal on top of the cooked food, is the process that stops microbes getting through to the food and contaminating it. The produce is densely packed into a sterilized container to expel any air pockets, then topped with liquid fat. Fat molecules are mostly long, straight hydrocarbon chains that pack neatly and clump together to form a solid, rigid lattice when the fat cools and congeals. This forms a hard barrier that oxygen can't penetrate – therefore any bacteria in the produce are starved of oxygen and can't thrive. The method was born of necessity in a time before refrigeration, but it still works. Using this traditional technique, potted confit duck (see left), for example, can keep for several weeks in a cool larder.

PRE-POTTING AND FAT CHOICE

If you are potting to preserve, then food should always be dried, salted, or cooked beforehand to kill or suppress harmful microorganisms. The produce must be in good condition before potting because any existing bacteria will be trapped under the fat barrier and can multiply. The choice of fat is also something to consider. Potting is the traditional way to store salt-cured meat that has been slowly cooked and then preserved in its own fat, but clarified butter is also an important fat used in potting. Having been heated and filtered to remove all milk solids, which become rancid over time when oxidized, clarified butter has an extended shelf life. The other benefit of using butter is that it is a vector for taste, facilitating the release of flavour compounds that aren't soluble in water.

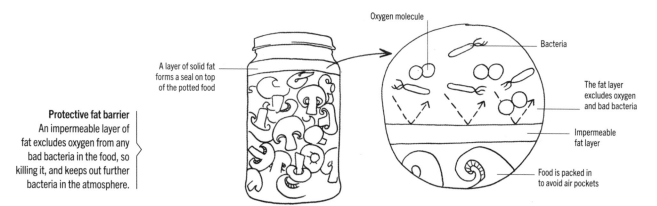

Protective fat barrier
An impermeable layer of fat excludes oxygen from any bad bacteria in the food, so killing it, and keeps out further bacteria in the atmosphere.

A layer of solid fat forms a seal on top of the potted food

Oxygen molecule

Bacteria

The fat layer excludes oxygen and bad bacteria

Impermeable fat layer

Food is packed in to avoid air pockets

THE PRACTICE

Potted Mushrooms

This woodland-inspired preserve is delicious served on hot toasted sourdough
with a poached egg or added to a risotto with a drizzle of truffle oil. The key is
to cook your mushrooms until they have caramelized and soaked up all the
flavour from your herbs and spices. Prepare enough clarified butter for a
thick protective layer.

Figure a.

Figure b.

Figure c.

MAKES

750ml (1¼-pint) jar

INGREDIENTS

150g (5½oz) salted butter
2 shallots, finely diced
1kg (2¼lb) mixed mushrooms,
    roughly chopped
2 garlic cloves, finely chopped
pinch of grated nutmeg
4 sprigs of thyme, leaves chopped,
    plus 1 sprig to garnish
50ml (3 tbsp) apple brandy or
    sherry
sea salt and cracked black pepper

EQUIPMENT

large frying pan or cast-iron skillet
small saucepan or butterpan
750ml (1¼-pint) glass jar,
    sterilized

Method

01 Melt 75g (2½oz) of the butter in a large frying pan or
    skillet and add your shallots, mushrooms, and garlic.
    Cook over a high heat until the shallots have softened
    and the mushrooms have started to brown (**fig. a**).

02 Meanwhile, slowly melt the remaining butter in a small
    saucepan or butterpan for 5–10 minutes and skim off
    the white, foamy milk solids from the surface using a
    slotted spoon. Set aside the clarified butter, away from
    the direct heat but keeping it warm so that it doesn't
    set while the mushrooms are cooking.

03 Reduce the heat under your mushrooms and add in
    the nutmeg and chopped thyme. Season to taste with
    about 1 teaspoon of salt and a pinch of black pepper.

04 After 5–10 minutes, add the brandy or sherry and
    flambé to burn off the alcohol. Then remove the
    mushrooms from the heat and pour into a glass
    jar (**fig. b**).

05 Press down the mushroom mixture with a spoon to
    expel any air pockets. Smooth the top and then pour
    over a generous layer of the clarified butter (**fig. c**).

06 Garnish the top of the clarified butter with a sprig of
    thyme. Allow to cool so the butter sets to form an
    impermeable barrier. Store in a cool cupboard for
    up to 4 weeks. After the butter seal has been broken,
    keep refrigerated and consume within 1 week.

EXPERT TIPS

You can blitz the mushrooms into
a spreadable paste before potting,
but I like the rustic texture of
mushrooms on toast.

———

Make clarified butter in a large
batch and store for up to 6 months
at room temperature or for 1 year
in the fridge. If stored at cooler
temperatures it will solidify, so you
will need to warm it up to liquefy it
again before pouring into pots.

———

You can blitz dried porcini
mushrooms into a powder and add
to warm clarified butter to make a
flavoured version. Cook over a low
heat for 3–4 minutes to release the
flavours and allow to cool as usual.
This flavoured butter can be used
for all kinds of potting.

THE POSSIBILITIES

Pots of Flavour

It doesn't get much better than spreading cold butter-topped treats onto a slice of hot toast. Go to town with potted food and your larder will quickly fill up with goodies.

SEAFOOD POTS

Fish and seafood were made for potting – and the recipes are now classics.

- Brown shrimp or crab **(fig. a)** flavoured with grated nutmeg get an extra lift when chilli, tarragon, or parsley are added to the mix.
- Potted trout **(fig. b)** and salmon are delicious. Poach the fish, then blitz into a smooth pâté. Season the butter with a pinch of mace, white pepper, cayenne pepper, and lemon juice.
- Try blitzing potted mussels into a smooth "mussel butter", then either use to cook with or serve with grilled fish.

Try … Potted crab (fig. c) Pick your crab and combine 250g (9oz) white and brown meat.

Mix well with ½ red chilli, deseeded and finely diced, 1 finely chopped garlic clove, the zest of 1 lemon, and 1 teaspoon of finely chopped parsley. Season well with a pinch each of sea salt and black pepper. Mix the crab with 50g (1¾oz) clarified butter and pour another 50g (1¾oz) over the top to seal the potted crab.

THE RIGHT STUFF

Use soft potted produce as a stuffing or croquette for a contrasting mouth-feel.

- Shredded potted duck with chestnut and orange zest is delicious stuffed into a cabbage leaf. Brush with walnut oil and roast in the oven until crispy.
- Form into croquettes or bonbons and coat with seasoned flour, beaten egg, and panko breadcrumbs, then deep-fry for 4–5 minutes until golden brown.

Figure a.

Figure b.

Figure c.

Figure d.

LUXURY LEFTOVERS

You can make potted meat from any leftover roast. This is a kind of English rillettes, and will keep for a month in the fridge.

- Mix chopped salt beef or mutton with clarified butter, cayenne, lemon zest, salt, pepper, and nutmeg, then pack the meat into a dish and top with clarified butter and a bay leaf. Serve with sourdough and chutney.
- Try turkey with mustard and leeks, roast chicken shredded and mixed with tarragon and dried apricot, or poached salmon with fresh dill and lemon zest.
- Serve potted ham with an acidic condiment like piccalilli (see pp.32–33) to cut through the richness or with crunchy pickles for a change of texture **(fig. d)**.

Try ... Potted ham Soften 2 diced onions in 50g (1¾oz) butter and add in the zest of 1 orange, 1 tablespoon of wholegrain mustard, 1 teaspoon of Dijon mustard, a pinch of ground cloves, 1 tablespoon of chopped thyme, and 100ml (3½fl oz) pork stock. Then shred in 500g (1lb 2oz) cooked ham hock. Stir well and transfer to small ramekins. Cover with clarified butter and keep refrigerated. Serve within 4 weeks.

CARCASS CARTEL

I use meat with an all-or-nothing attitude, and potting is ideal for nose-to-tail cooking.

- Make potted tongue with mace butter, the go-to spice of English potted meats and fish.
- Try duck liver and redcurrant, potted with a bay-leaf-infused clarified butter and served with walnuts and a bitter salad.
- My dad loves to make confit gizzards and hearts, preserved in duck fat. Add to stews or flash finish on a chargrill.

"

The potential to bring a fresh perspective to this ancient preserving method always fills me with excitement. You get to play at being a food historian while challenging yourself with new ideas.

"

CURING

Project 18
DRY CURING

Preserved morsels of mineral-crusted delight.

SKILL LEVEL Medium–
hard: balancing the curing
and air-drying time to achieve
a perfectly preserved product
takes practice.

TIMINGS 1 hour–2 weeks
curing; 4 weeks–12 months
air-drying.

Miracle cures
Meat, fish, and even egg
yolks can be preserved in
aromatic salt cures.

Salt Preservation

Since ancient times people have been using salt-based cures to preserve meat and fish. The chemical properties of salt trigger a unique reaction in raw food when left in contact with it, enhancing flavours and drawing out moisture via osmosis to suppress the growth of bacteria. Salt-preservation techniques may have changed over the years, but the science behind them remains the same and is as useful today as it was a thousand years ago.

PREVENTING BOTULISM

The salt in a dry cure inhibits the growth of food-spoiling microorganisms by drawing out their cellular moisture via osmosis and thereby denaturing them. As water moves out of microbial cells and salt moves in to balance the salinity on either side, the dehydrated bacteria cells begin to die off. As the risk of unwanted microbes decreases, beneficial lactobacillus bacteria can flourish and, fed by the sugar that often goes into a cure, generate lactic acid. This inhibits bad bacteria even more, and causes the lactic tang in some dry-cured products. Smoking or air-drying are often used as well as dry-curing to boost the preservation process. Smoking protects the surface with antibacterial chemicals while air-drying further reduces moisture.

SALTS OF THE EARTH

Salts are complex minerals made up of sodium, magnesium, calcium, iodine, and potassium, and the varying levels of these elements in each type give them their distinctive flavours. Sodium chloride (standard table salt) is the active preserving agent in the curing process, but it's never found naturally in isolation; it's surrounded by a blend of over 66 other minerals, all with their own beneficial properties and flavours. Salts enhance food by dissolving in the mouth and increasing the salinity of saliva; this increases the connectivity between food and our taste buds, as the charged ions in the salt act as a conductor for the flavour. The more salts in action, the greater the number of connections and the more amplified the flavours become.

Bacterial dehydration
Salt crystals in a cure kill off bacteria by drawing out their moisture through osmosis, so collapsing the cells.

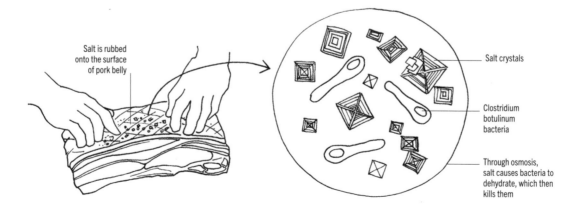

Salt is rubbed onto the surface of pork belly

Salt crystals

Clostridium botulinum bacteria

Through osmosis, salt causes bacteria to dehydrate, which then kills them

THE PRACTICE

Gravlax

A traditional gravlax cure is flavoured with lots of chopped dill and black pepper, but this recipe puts a colourful twist on the Scandinavian classic with the addition of beetroot, which turns the fish a vivid purple. Not only does the finished dish look visually impressive, but the whisky and orange add a real depth of flavour.

MAKES

750g (1lb 10oz) gravlax

INGREDIENTS

750g (1lb 10oz) side of salmon,
    skinned and deboned
For the cure
75ml (2½fl oz) whisky
4 tbsp salt
2 tbsp granulated sugar
zest and juice of 1 orange
2 tbsp chopped dill
1 tbsp crushed black peppercorns
1 tbsp crushed coriander seeds
1 beetroot, peeled and grated

EQUIPMENT

large non-reactive container
    (stainless steel, ceramic,
    glass, or plastic)
press lid or plates
weights or tins

Method

01   To make the cure, mix the whisky, salt, sugar, orange zest and juice, dill, and spices in a bowl, then combine with the grated beetroot **(fig. a)**.

02   Place the side of salmon in a large non-reactive container and rub the cure into the fish thoroughly on all sides **(fig. b)**.

03   Apply some pressure on top of the fish to speed up the curing process. I have made a lid that fits inside my curing dish **(fig. c)**, then I simply add tins from the larder on top to weigh it down. Alternatively, wrap the salmon tightly in baking parchment and press between 2 plates with weights on top (again, evenly spaced tins from the larder are ideal). Leave to cure in the fridge, at below 5°C (41°F), for 36 hours. Check on it occasionally and pour off any liquid brine as it drains from the fish.

04   Scrape off the cure and rinse the salmon under cold running water. Gently pat dry with kitchen paper.

05   Slice the side of salmon thinly on an angle and serve. Store in the fridge for 1 week.

EXPERT TIPS

Reduce the curing time by 12 hours if you want a softer texture.

———

Always use sashimi-grade fish or, to be super safe, freeze the fish for 24 hours before starting the curing process, to kill off any parasites.

———

Once the fish is cured and patted dry, try adding a crust of red chilli flakes, chopped dill, crushed black pepper, and coriander for a warming play on fish pastrami.

Figure a.

Figure b.

Figure c.

Figure a.

MAKES

750g (1lb 10oz) bresaola

INGREDIENTS

1kg (2¼lb) silverside beef
For the cure
1 tbsp black peppercorns
1 tsp juniper berries
1 tsp grated garlic
25g (scant 1oz) sea salt
    flakes, or curing salt (see
    Expert Tips, opposite)
25g (scant 1oz) brown sugar
35ml (1fl oz) red wine

EQUIPMENT

pestle and mortar
large, airtight, food-safe
    container, such as a
    plastic, ceramic, or
    glass box, or resealable
    plastic bag
muslin or cheesecloth
butcher's hook (optional)

THE PRACTICE

Bresaola

Bresaola is air-dried, salted beef that is normally made from silverside, but
you can also try it with a loin of venison. This simple cure is understated and
classic, allowing the subtle tang of fermented beef to ride out the warm wave
of peppercorns and red-wine tannins. Try serving with Parmesan shavings,
radicchio, and figs pickled in red wine vinegar.

Figure b.

Figure c.

Figure d.

Method

01   Start by preparing your beef. Good fat marbling throughout will keep the bresaola moist and tender, but trim off any sinew and fat from the exterior **(fig. a)**. For extra-safe curing, you can freeze the beef beforehand to kill off any parasites.

02   Next, make the cure. Grind the peppercorns and juniper berries in a pestle and mortar with the garlic **(fig. b)** and mix well with the salt and brown sugar.

03   Place the meat in an airtight, food-safe container and rub half the cure into the surface of the beef until evenly coated **(fig. c)**. Add the red wine to the container and roll the meat in the mixture until evenly coated. Store the remaining cure in a sealed jar in the fridge.

04   Next, seal the container and refrigerate at under 5°C (41°F) for 2 weeks. Turn the meat daily for the first week, then pat dry with kitchen paper and rub again with the reserved half of the cure. Return to the fridge in the sealed container, and turn every couple of days during the second week of curing. Each day pour off the liquid that is drawn from the meat. Less and less will come out each day and the meat texture will get firmer as the colour of the flesh gets darker.

05   After 2 weeks, take the meat out of the container and pat dry with kitchen paper to remove the cure. Then weigh the beef and make a note of the figure.

06   Wrap the meat loosely in muslin or cheesecloth and secure with string **(fig. d)**. Hang it (from a butcher's hook, or similar) in a cool, well-ventilated place away from direct sunlight to air-dry for 2–4 weeks.

07   Weigh the meat every few days while it is air-drying. It will be ready when its weight has reduced by over 35 per cent due to moisture loss. When the target weight has been reached, unwrap the meat, slice thinly, and serve. Store in an airtight container in the fridge and eat within 2 weeks.

EXPERT TIPS

Curing salt contains nitrates and nitrites to help prevent botulism, a dangerous toxin that develops in poorly preserved food. I don't use curing salt because nitrites are potentially carcinogenic. I ensure food safety by keeping equipment clean, curing slowly in cold temperatures, and using top-quality ingredients, but if worried, you can replace sea salt with curing salt.

The key to effective air-drying is good airflow, a fairly constant temperature of 6–12°C (50–65°F), and avoiding direct contact with moisture in an environment that is 60–80 per cent humidity.

THE PRACTICE

Salted Lemons

This umami-rich citrus preserve is incredibly versatile. It can be used as a condiment, cooked in stews and tagines, fried with padrón peppers or added to a humble hummus for extra complexity. My favourite kitchen hack is to add a few slices of cured lemon to mash or to a white fish cooked *en papillote* – this both seasons the dishes and gives them an added zing.

MAKES

1-litre (1¾-pint) jar

INGREDIENTS

6 unwaxed lemons
8 tbsp sea salt flakes
1 tbsp pink peppercorns
4 sprigs of rosemary
2 sprigs of thyme

EQUIPMENT

1-litre (1¾-pint) glass
    preserving jar, sterilized

Method

01 Prepare 5 of the lemons by cutting a cross lengthways
down the centre of each **(fig. a)**, but being careful not
to cut all the way through.

02 Work 1 tablespoon of salt per lemon into the grooves
of each one until they are evenly coated **(fig. b)**.

03 Press the salted lemons down into a glass preserving
jar, packing them as tightly as you can, then add the
remaining salt.

04 Seal the jar **(fig. c)** and leave it to sit in a cool cupboard
for 1 week. The lemon juice and brine will start to seep
out of the lemons and into the jar.

05 After a week, add the aromatics, cover with the juice
of the 1 remaining lemon, then reseal the jar.

06 Leave the lemons to cure for 3 weeks, shaking the
jar once a week to evenly distribute the aromatics.

07 Store the cured lemons in a cupboard for up to 6
months. Once opened, keep in the fridge and either
cover with more lemon juice or with olive oil, as
needed, after use. Eat within 2 weeks.

EXPERT TIPS

Meyer lemons are the best type to
use for preservation, but you can
try the same method with limes or
bergamot lemons.

———

Use unwaxed lemons if you can, as
you will eat the rind. Alternatively,
if you can only find waxed lemons,
scrub them under very hot water
to remove wax before you start.

———

Use cured lemons sparingly, as
you will quickly discover that they
impart a sophisticated flavour
that verges on intense.

———

Experiment with your aromatics
– try adding cinnamon, bay, or
chilli flakes to the cure.

Figure a.

Figure b.

Figure c.

THE POSSIBILITIES

A Cure for Everything

Curing is a way to change radically your everyday food into salty gold and fill the kitchen with culinary gemstones. You will soon be obsessed with the magic of this method.

DUCK CHARCUTERIE

Cured duck goes extremely well with orange or redcurrants, but these classic combinations can sometimes feel a bit old-fashioned.

- Try cured duck with a walnut, pear, and celery salad for a twist on a classic Waldorf.
- Serve duck ham with melon and blue cheese, or wrapped around a slice of fig with honey and thyme for a delicious tapas dish.
- Carve wafer-thin slices of duck prosciutto and serve on grilled sourdough with rocket and redcurrant jelly.

Try ... Duck prosciutto (fig. a) Take 2 duck breasts and trim off any loose fat, then prick the skin several times with a skewer about halfway into the breast. Rub in a cure made with the zest of 1 orange, 2 crushed star anise, 100g (3½oz) sea salt, 40g (1¼oz) brown sugar, 1 teaspoon of chopped thyme, and 1 teaspoon of whole pink peppercorns. Place the duck breasts in a sealed container or resealable bag. Cover the duck with any remaining cure and leave in the fridge for 4 days. Wash off the cure and pat dry before carving thinly.

BRING HOME THE BACON

Bacon takes time and planning – dry-curing pork belly in sea salt and brown sugar **(fig. b)** takes 1 week – so I tend to work ahead, with cuts at different stages: some in the fridge curing while others are air-drying.

Figure a.

Figure b.

Figure c.

Figure d.

- Mix juniper berries, pink peppercorns, and chilli flakes into the cure for a top flavour hit.
- Dry-cured bacon contains far less water than much commercial bacon, so it crisps up nicely for a classic English breakfast.
- Bacon chilli jam is a sweet, salty preserve made with cooked diced bacon, chipotle, and sweet vinegar. Cook down until sticky and serve with decadent bacon butties.

SOFT CURED

Dry-curing is not just for meat and fish. Use it to add flavour and firmness to softer foods, too.

- Try soft-curing egg yolks with seaweed salt **(fig. c).** These are delicious with kedgeree, soup, or charcoal-cured trout **(fig. d)**. Beetroot or beef tartare are also fantastic with a cured egg yolk for a salty umami hit.
- Cured hearts and gizzards from ducks and chickens are an excellent way to make the most of offal. Try dry-curing and then braising slowly in red wine.
- Dry-cured roe from grey mullet is delicious grated over pasta. Often called *bottarga*, it works particularly well with a clam linguine instead of Parmesan for a rich, salty garnish.

Try ... Seaweed-cured egg yolks Place 4 egg yolks on a lined tray. Mix 2 tablespoons of sea salt flakes and 1 teaspoon of seaweed flakes, then sprinkle over the eggs. Cover lightly with cling film, being careful not to break the yolks, and leave in the fridge for 4–5 hours. The yolks will still be soft but easy to handle.

❝

Rubbing in salt flakes and sugar crystals and then observing the change in the ingredients encapsulates the tactile magic and metamorphosis of the artisan kitchen.

❞

> "
> *Salt is a wonder ingredient, transforming the texture of food, preserving it, and adding intense flavour. It's an ancient preservative, but we still use it – for good reason.*
> "

Project 19
WET CURING

Succulent cuts of meat or fish submerged in a briny concoction.

SKILL LEVEL Easy.

TIMINGS 30 minutes prep;
5 hours–5 days wet curing.

Meat immersion
Gammon submerged in a
spiced brine is the first
step towards delicious
ham (see pp.172–73).

THE SCIENCE

Saline Solutions

Wet curing is similar to the marinating process but works without acid.
Meat or fish are immersed in a strong brine solution, which draws out
moisture from the food via osmosis, and preserves it. At the same time, the
herbs and spices in the brine penetrate the food to impart bucket-loads of
salty flavour, while the liquid in the brine prevents dehydration, keeping
the meat moist and juicy with a butter-soft texture.

PRESERVATION AND FLAVOUR

Submerging produce in brine creates an
anaerobic environment. The lack of oxygen
prevents oxidation, while the salt in the brine
draws out moisture from the microbes via
osmosis, concentrating flavour and dehydrating
(and thus destroying) bad bacteria. As salt
dissolves in water, it penetrates deep into meat
membranes, even in larger cuts. This prevents
localized "hot-spots", where the cure is uneven
due to the varying thickness of the meat, which
can be a problem with dry cures. The movement
of salt from an area of high concentration to low
during osmosis results in equilibrium, achieving
even salinity throughout – in other words,
perfectly seasoned meat inside and out. Some
recipes will require you to carry out a sweet brine
as well, in which the sugar content is higher than
the salt; this balances the saltiness, but also feeds
the growth of lactobacillus – a beneficial bacteria
that helps both flavour and preservation.

TEXTURE

Meat is about 70 per cent water, and around
30 per cent of a protein's moisture can be lost
during cooking. However, despite drawing
moisture out of meat, wet curing also keeps it
juicy by increasing the water-holding capacity
of its cells. The dissolved salt ions bind the
water in the muscle fibres more tightly together,
helping them resist the shrinkage that squeezes
juice out when cooked. The salt in brine also
helps to dissolve the tough proteins in meat,
resulting in a juicy, tender texture.

Brining
Submerging meat in a brine
keeps it moist by modifying
the muscle fibres to become
more moisture retentive,
even once cooked.

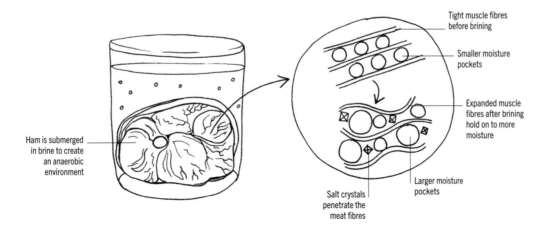

Ham is submerged
in brine to create
an anaerobic
environment

Tight muscle fibres
before brining

Smaller moisture
pockets

Expanded muscle
fibres after brining
hold on to more
moisture

Salt crystals
penetrate the
meat fibres

Larger moisture
pockets

THE PRACTICE

Ham

Self-praise is no form of recommendation, but this really is a great ham recipe. My secret to succulent slices is a simple three-stage process: a spiced brine, slow-cooking, and a sweet glaze. Making your own ham from scratch gives you the flexibility to add some real flavour deep in the meat – and there's nothing more satisfying than carving and serving this beauty.

Figure a.

Figure b.

Figure c.

MAKES

1kg (2¼lb) ham

INGREDIENTS

1kg (2¼lb) skinless gammon joint
20 cloves
For the cure
5 litres (8¾ pints) water
500g (1lb 2oz) sea salt
750g (1lb 10oz) caster sugar
2 bay leaves
6 sprigs of thyme
1 tsp yellow mustard seeds
1 tsp black peppercorns
2 star anise
4 cloves
2 cardamom pods, crushed
For the mirepoix
1 carrot, peeled and coarsely
    chopped
1 stick of celery, coarsely chopped
1 shallot, peeled and halved
1 bay leaf
For the glaze
2 tbsp orange marmalade
1 tsp mustard powder

EQUIPMENT

brining container (see Expert Tips,
    right)
large stock pan

Method

01 First, make the cure. Boil the water and pour into the brining container **(fig. a)**, then add the salt and sugar and dissolve. Add your herbs and spices, then leave the cure to infuse as it cools.

02 Submerge your gammon in the sweet brine, seal the container, then leave in the fridge for 2–3 days (2 days will have a good impact; 3 days will fully infuse the flavour and brine the meat throughout).

03 Remove the ham from the brine, pat dry with kitchen paper, then submerge in a large stock pan of cold water. Add the mirepoix ingredients to the pan **(fig. b)** and cook at a low simmer for 2–3 hours.

04 Remove the ham from the pan when the fat starts to separate from the meat. Allow to drain and cool slightly on a wire rack set over a tray to catch any liquid. Preheat the oven to 180°C (350°F/Gas 4).

05 Score the fat in a diamond pattern and insert a clove at each cross section **(fig. c)**. Next, make the glaze by mixing the marmalade and mustard powder in a pan and bringing to the boil, then brush the glaze generously over the scored ham.

06 Cook in the oven in a large roasting tray for 20 minutes until the fat is golden. Once cooled, slice and serve. Store in the fridge for 1 week.

EXPERT TIPS

You will need a non-reactive container to seal the solution and the meat while curing. The easiest option is to use a resealable plastic bag laid on a tray. For a large cut of meat you may need to use an ice box, washtub, or even plastic bin (if this won't fit in your fridge, add ice to the brine solution instead of water). Keep food submerged and refrigerated at below 5°C (41°F).

———

Don't reuse brine solutions, and always use a solution of at least 4 per cent salt – beyond 6 per cent the meat may become unpalatable. Change the solution regularly if curing a large cut of meat.

———

A technical way to measure the strength of your brine is to use a salinometer or brinometer, which consist of a float with a stem attached. The reading is taken at the level the stem floats in the brine.

———

To reduce the saltiness of brined meat, soak it in fresh water for 1 hour after the wet-curing stage and before cooking.

THE POSSIBILITIES

Brine Benefits

Brining is a one-way ticket to flavour-town. Preparing leaner meats in a wet cure keeps them moist, seasons them, and add flavours from the inside out.

LEAN BUT JUICY

I brine most meats before sticking them on the BBQ, as it keeps them moist and tender.

- Deep-fry wings, drumsticks, and thighs that have been brined first. Add Cajun spices to the brine before coating in a spiced batter.
- Pork loin or non-fatty cuts work well if you brine them first. Add some spices and herbs to the brine for a more rounded flavour.
- Whole birds are slightly more difficult to brine but still worth the effort. A brined chicken or turkey takes on more flavour from a rub or a smoker and cooks better than when it's been simply marinated.

Try ... Bourbon-brined chicken Prepare your brine by mixing 250ml (8fl oz) water, 250ml (8fl oz) bourbon, 150ml (5fl oz) maple syrup, 75g (2½oz) salt, 4 cloves, the zest of 1 orange, 1 bay leaf, and 1 sprig of thyme in a large jug. Place a 1kg (2¼lb) chicken in a large plastic container or resealable bag and cover with the brine. Seal and leave in the fridge to cure for 6–12 hours. Turn the chicken every hour or two for an even cure. Pat dry with kitchen paper and cover with a spiced rub of paprika, thyme, garlic powder, onion powder, black pepper, and sea salt. Preheat a hot smoker or BBQ to 200°C (390°F) and cook for 45 minutes until the skin is golden and the juices run clear.

Figure a.

Figure b.

Figure c.

BUTTERMILK BRINING

Add salt to buttermilk for a brine that works as a conventional wet cure, keeps meat super juicy, and also adds a tangy flavour.

- Buttermilk-brined chicken wings are simple but hugely satisfying. Coat them in spiced cornflakes and fry for classic crispy chicken, or for a curried version fry the brined wings in an Indian spiced butter **(fig. a)**.
- Try monkfish soaked in buttermilk for 1–2 hours, before brining in a salted-water wet cure. Then fry in a Cajun spiced batter and serve with waffles and a fried egg **(fig. b)**.

Try ... Buttermilk-brined chicken wings
Combine 500ml (16fl oz) buttermilk with 4 teaspoons of salt and soak 750kg (1lb 10oz) chicken wings in the mixture **(fig. c)**. Seal in an airtight container and refrigerate for 4 hours or overnight. Drain off the buttermilk, pat the wings dry with kitchen paper, and dip them first in 4 tablespoons of seasoned flour, then in 2 beaten eggs, then in 100g (3½oz) crushed cornflakes spiced with 2 tablespoons of Cajun spices. Fry in hot oil at 180°C (356°F) for 6–8 minutes until the chicken reaches 75°C (167°F) inside (use a meat thermometer to check this). Serve with hot sauce.

A wet cure is doing the practical job of retaining moisture while cooking, but it also has the power to weave big flavours into food.

SANDWICH HEAVEN

Brisket is a fatty cut of beef, full of connective tissue. When wet cured for 1 week in a spiced brine and then slow-boiled over 3–4 hours in fresh water, it makes for really moist salt beef.

- My favourite combination is hot-smoked salt beef (see pp.204–05) in a bagel with mustard mayo, dill pickles, and sauerkraut **(fig. d)**.
- Salt beef makes superb croquettes or nuggets. Shred the brined meat, form into balls, then coat in a beer batter and deep-fry.

Figure d.

Project 20
SAUSAGES

Salted bangers linking juicy, sweet, and spicy in one sentence.

SKILL LEVEL Easy–
medium: if using a sausage
machine, this is painless;
if working manually,
sausages can be tricky.

TIMINGS 30 minutes–
1 hour for mincing and filling;
4–6 weeks fermenting.

Fermented chorizo
Spiced minced pork is
stuffed into casings and
tied off into individual
sausages with string.

THE SCIENCE

Minced Meat

Sausage-making is both a science and an art. The principles are straightforward, but the intricacies of fat content, meat ratio, casing size, and fermentation time can make the difference between a wonderful sausage and an average one. These long, slender links of mince can be made fresh and then cooked, or fermented and eaten without cooking – the skills to produce them are the same; only the ingredients and the process differ.

FRESH

The most common meat for sausage-making is ground pork or beef, but you can also use lamb, duck, venison, or even fish. Casings of varying diameters are usually made from either pork, lamb, or beef intestines, and there are now artificial casings available, too. In general, a good sausage requires 25–30 per cent fat content or it will taste dry, so try to use a mix of lean and fattier cuts – shoulder and belly work well. The fat helps to baste the sausage from the inside as it cooks, while added breadcrumbs (rusk) help to keep sausages moist and retain succulence as they cook. The mark of a good sausage is if most of the fat and juices stay in the sausage rather than escaping, so for best results, aim for 18–20 per cent rusk in your recipes.

FERMENTED

To make fermented sausages, meat is minced, spiced, and salted to dry-cure and preserve it. Once filled, the casings are punctured to remove any air pockets that could adversely affect fermentation. They are then air-dried to allow the moisture drawn out by the salting process to evaporate, creating an inhospitable environment for bad bacteria. Subjecting sausages to microbial fermentation while they air-dry lowers their pH level from around 5.8 down to 5.3–4.6, as the lactic acid bacteria convert the sugars in the cure to lactic acid. This not only suppresses bad bacteria, but it also lends the sausages an enhanced tangy flavour profile. Smoking is often the final hurdle. This adds flavour, but also further inhibits unwelcome microbes.

Meat content
For a successful sausage that remains moist once cooked, the ideal ratio in the sausage mix is 50% meat, 30% fat, and 20% rusk.

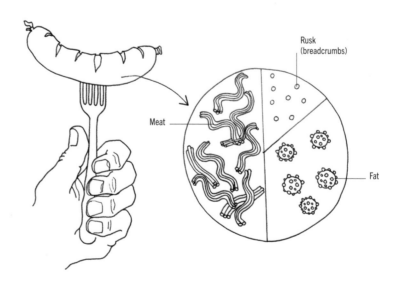

Rusk (breadcrumbs)

Meat

Fat

THE PRACTICE

Chorizo

I made my first chorizo sausages around the same age that I first tasted red wine – and I haven't looked back! For me, chorizo is the gateway into fermented sausages. It is colourful, spicy, and packed with flavours that intensify with fermentation. It's ideal served with a hard goat's cheese, honey, and thyme; stirred into a hot gumbo with shrimp; or plated up with pink pickled onions, dill and turmeric cucumber, and fermented red cabbage.

Figure a.

MAKES

6 sausages

INGREDIENTS

1kg (2¼lb) skinless pork shoulder
1kg (2¼lb) skinless pork belly
500g (1lb 2oz) pork fat
75g (2½oz) sea salt, or curing salt
    (see Expert Tips, right)
15g (½oz) demerara sugar
8 garlic cloves, finely chopped
2 tbsp smoked paprika
1 tbsp fennel seeds
50ml (2fl oz) red wine

EQUIPMENT

mincer and sausage-filling machine
    (optional – see Expert Tips,
    right)
35–50mm (1½–2in) x 1m (39in)
    hog casings
skewer or cocktail stick
butcher's hooks (optional)
muslin or cheesecloth

Method

01 If you have a mincer, chop the pork shoulder and belly meat into 2.5cm (1in) cubes **(fig. a)**, then grind the chopped meat in the mincer using a 6–8mm (¼–½in) plate. If you don't have a mincer, buy some pork mince or ask a butcher to mince the pork for you.

02 Finely dice the pork fat and place in a large bowl, then add the salt, sugar, garlic, spices, and pork mince. Knead together, working the ingredients into the mince, then mix in the red wine and mince the mixture for a second time **(fig. b)** or pulse in a food processor. Soak the casings in a bowl of cold water for 10 minutes, then, using a sausage-filling machine, feed the sausage mix into the casings **(fig. c)**. Twist off the sausages into 20–30cm (8–12in) links and tie off with string.

03 Prick each sausage with a skewer or cocktail stick to allow any air to escape before fermentation **(fig. d)**, making sure the casings don't tear. Next, weigh the sausages and note down the figure.

04 Hang the sausages from a butcher's hook or similar in a cool, well-ventilated place, making sure they aren't touching, and leave for 4–6 weeks to ferment and air-dry. Weigh them every few days – for a semi-dry sausage, they will be ready when they have lost 20 per cent of their weight. Before eating, clean off any white mould that has formed on the chorizo with a 1:1 vinegar and water solution using a piece of muslin. Once cut, store in the fridge and eat within 2 weeks.

EXPERT TIPS

A combined mincer and sausage-filling machine will save you time and energy. Look for one with different-width grinding plates: 10mm (½in) for coarse; 6mm (¼in) for medium, or 4.5mm (⅛in) for fine mince. Often you will need to mince twice. If you do need to fill sausages manually, a funnel and a spatula are your best bet.

———

Curing salts are used in commercial sausages to prevent botulism, which can be fatal. I avoid them as they contain nitrates and nitrites, which are potentially carcinogenic. Slow, nitrite-free curing at cold temperatures, using the best ingredients and clean equipment, is my preference, but you can replace sea salt with curing salt if you prefer.

———

Reduce the amount of salt to 2 teaspoons, so that you are seasoning the mince rather than curing it, and omit the air-drying process for a delicious fresh chorizo sausage. Keep refrigerated and enjoy cooked within 7 days.

Figure b.

Figure c.

Figure d.

THE PRACTICE

Seafood Salami

Ever since I tried Portuguese *mojama* – a salt-cured tuna speciality – I've wanted to try making my own seafood salami. This idea has become more popular among chefs, artisans, and charcuterie experts recently and the scope for experimentation is exciting. Cook the salami after curing it first, then serve with crisp courgette fritters, tartare sauce, and lemon wedges.

Figure a.

Figure b.

Figure c.

MAKES

2 large sausages

INGREDIENTS

200g (7oz) squid
750g (1lb 10oz) cod, salmon,
    and smoked haddock
50g (1¾oz) sun-dried tomatoes
20g (¾oz) Himalayan salt
1 tbsp capers
1 tsp pink peppercorns
zest of 1 lemon
1 tbsp chopped dill

EQUIPMENT

mincer and sausage-filling
    machine (optional)
38mm (1½in) x 50cm (19½in)
    hog casings

Method

01 Finely chop your squid and set aside, then chop the
fish into 2.5cm (1in) pieces. Finely chop the sun-dried
tomatoes as well **(fig. a)**. Then, if you have a mincer,
mince the chopped fish, tomatoes, salt, capers, and
peppercorns with a medium 6mm (¼in) plate.
Alternatively, blitz in a food processor.

02 In a bowl, work the diced squid, lemon zest, and
dill into the fish mince with your hands, mixing well
(fig. b). Use a sausage-filling machine to fill your hog
casings if you have one; alternatively, fill them using a
funnel and spatula. Once filled, tie the casings with
string into 2 large sausages **(fig. c)**.

03 Store the sausages in the fridge for 48 hours to allow
the flavours to develop, then steam in a pan of boiling
water for 5–10 minutes until the fish is cooked
through and opaque; serve warm.

EXPERT TIPS

Cold smoking (see pp.188–98) this
seafood salami over oak or apple
sawdust for 6–12 hours should
extend the shelf life to 7–10 days.
Keep refrigerated after smoking
and once sliced, eat within 2 days.

———

Follow these same principles to try
making your own octopus chorizo
or salmon belly bacon. Cure fresh
fish with 2–3 per cent salt for
fermentation, then hang in the
fridge at under 5°C (41°F) to air-dry
for 48 hours before cooking.

———

Casings taste neutral and won't
affect the flavour of sausages.
They will keep in the fridge in a salt
brine for about 1 month, and if
dry-packed will last in the fridge for
a year. They can also be frozen.

THE POSSIBILITIES

Sizzling Bangers

There's a sausage for everyone. They also provide a superb opportunity to avoid waste by making a tasty comfort food, so get creative with different meats and vegetables.

SPREADABLE SAUSAGE

'Nduja is a cured sausage from southern Italy. It's spicy, spreadable, and versatile.

- 'Nduja is delicious on pizza with mozzarella or spread inside toasted ciabatta sandwiches.
- Use it to stuff courgette flowers with a mellow heat, then serve with fig oil and heritage tomatoes **(fig. a)**.
- 'Nduja is beautiful when used to enrich a sausage roll with fiery heat, or stirred into a bolognese ragù or other stew to spice them up.

Try ... 'Nduja Soak 14cm (5½in) x 1m (39in) ox bung casings in warm water for 30 minutes, then mince 275g (10oz) Calabrian peperoncini piccanti, 500g (1lb 2oz) chopped pork shoulder and belly, 500g (1lb 2oz) pork fat, and 30g (1oz) sea salt (or curing salt, see p.179) in a sausage-making machine. Mince twice, once coarsely and then with a fine 4.5mm (¼in) plate, for a richly spiced purée **(fig. b)**. Fill the casings, then tie with string into 2 large sausages. Hang for 4 weeks in a cool, well-ventilated place. Once sliced, keep in the fridge and use within 4 weeks.

SPICY MERGUEZ

The coiled, spicy merguez lamb sausage **(fig. c)** originated in the Middle East and is popular all over Europe, especially in France.

Figure a.

Figure b.

Figure c.

Figure d.

- Grill over charcoal and serve with tabbouleh. Go super spicy by making it with extra chilli and harissa paste, or keep it lighter and aromatic with cumin seeds and rose petals.
- Serve with a slow-cooked tagine of vegetables garnished with chopped mint and coriander.
- Try an Algerian-style hot dog by serving with minted yogurt and cumin-pickled carrot slaw.

MEAT-FREE SAUSAGES

Sausages can be vegetarian inside and out – simply stuff with veg and use artificial casings.

- Mix beetroot, apricot, and harissa with mint and couscous for a twist on a merguez.
- Mince some tofu and then pair with a selection of herbs for a Cumberland-style veggie banger. Sage, nutmeg, parsley, and mustard make a great winter warmer.
- Mince chickpeas, onion bhaji, sweet potato, and cumin seeds for an Indian-style sausage.
- Green vegetable sausages can redefine a classic meat-and-two-veg meal. Try them with onion gravy and mashed potato.

Try ... Green sausages Combine 200g (7oz) cooked quinoa with 150g (5½oz) grated courgette, 150g (5½oz) spinach, and 100g (3½oz) shredded kale in a mincer or food processor, then add 2 finely sliced spring onions and 100g (3½oz) drained chickpeas. Mix in 1 tablespoon of grated fresh root ginger, 1 tablespoon of grated garlic, 1 tablespoon of chopped mint leaves, and 1 tablespoon of fresh coriander, and season to taste with salt and pepper. Fill artificial casings with the mixture and twist into linked sausages **(fig. d)**. Fry in a drizzle of oil for 5–6 minutes or roast in the oven for 15 minutes at 180°C (350°F/Gas 4).

The sausage is the ultimate kitchen hero. Whether bringing together disparate, neglected cuts of meat, or a panoply of seasonal vegetables, the result is almost always a banger for taste.

I first made sausages from our own pigs over 15 years ago and it was a revelation to see how many parts of the animal could be put into a sausage. They are the perfect representation of nose-to-tail eating – everything except the oink.

SMOKING

———

Project 21
COLD SMOKING

Uncooked cured, fermented, or dried produce infused with cool smoke.

SKILL LEVEL Medium:
the challenge is to avoid
over-smoking and drying
out the produce too much.

TIMINGS 30 minutes
preparation; 2–24 hours
smoking.

**Cold-smoked
kippers and garlic**
Kippers are usually
cold-smoked herring, but
I like to kipper mackerel
when it's in good supply.

THE SCIENCE

Cold-smoke Infusion

Cold smoking is indirectly applying smoke to food at a low temperature of 15–30°C (60–90°F), so that it is infused with smoky notes but does not cook. For this reason, fish, meat, and vegetables are always fermented, cured, or dried first. The smoke not only imparts immense flavour, but further dries the food and helps preserve the otherwise raw produce by coating the surface in a protective layer of antibacterial molecules.

MOLECULAR PRESERVATION

Smoke is an aerosol made up of solid particles, liquid droplets, and gases created by the process of combustion. In the cocktail emitted from burning wood there are hundreds of volatile molecules, including phenols, formaldehyde, and acetic acid, which all have strong antibacterial qualities; and eugenol, a chemical compound that also has strong antimicrobial properties, as well as being a powerful antioxidant. These useful molecules settle on the surface of the food and form a tasty outer layer that serves as a protective shield against spoilage from moulds and bacteria. Wood smoke also has a low pH level of 2.5, and this acidity only adds to the inhospitable environment for microbes.

WOOD-SMOKE FLAVOUR

The flavours imparted by cold smoking will change from wood to wood, depending on their proportions of cellulose, hemicellulose, and lignin – the three main compounds in wood. During combustion, the glucose in cellulose

and hemicellulose produces sweet, caramel-like flavour molecules, while lignin breaks down into phenolics, which carry spicy notes of cloves and vanilla. These aromatic particles fly through the smoke vapour and condense when they come into contact with food. This process can be aided by air-drying beforehand, which forms a tacky coating of proteins on the food's surface, known as the pellicle. The pellicle helps smoke particles adhere and bond to the food's surface, providing a protective and flavoursome outer layer.

Smoke flavour profiles
The main components of combusted wood – lignin, cellulose, and hemicellulose – convey different flavour particles in the smoke.

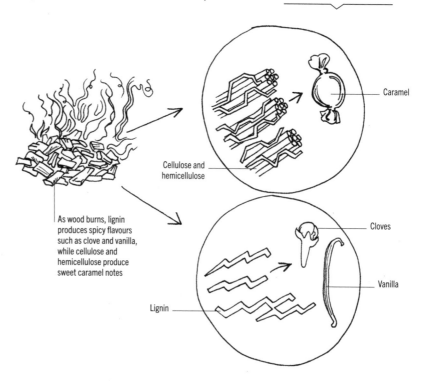

As wood burns, lignin produces spicy flavours such as clove and vanilla, while cellulose and hemicellulose produce sweet caramel notes

Caramel

Cellulose and hemicellulose

Cloves

Vanilla

Lignin

THE PRACTICE

Make a Cold Smoker

Smokers come in all shapes and sizes, and there are now a wide range available to buy ready-made to suit any budget. Alternatively, they can easily be built at home from scratch. In their simplest form, cold smokers just need a brick oven or firebox to house the fire, and a separate smoke chamber connected by a flue to hold the smoke and the food being smoked.

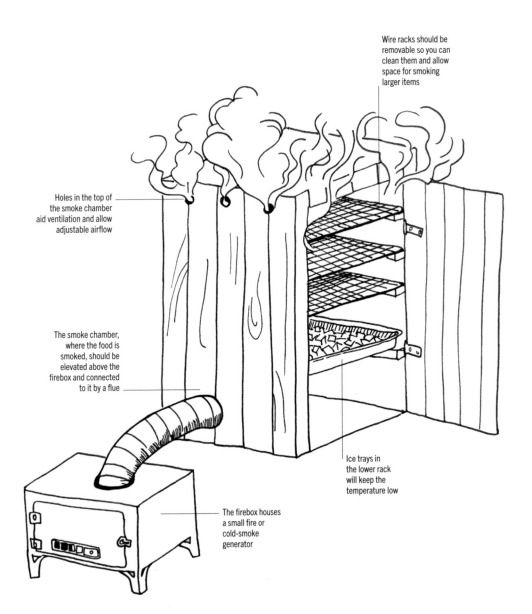

Wire racks should be removable so you can clean them and allow space for smoking larger items

Holes in the top of the smoke chamber aid ventilation and allow adjustable airflow

The smoke chamber, where the food is smoked, should be elevated above the firebox and connected to it by a flue

Ice trays in the lower rack will keep the temperature low

The firebox houses a small fire or cold-smoke generator

EQUIPMENT

For the firebox

small wood-burning stove (optional)

20kg (3 stone) mortar (4 parts sand:1 part cement)

12–24 fire bricks

15 x 20cm (6 x 8in) metal-hinged pizza-oven frame and door

flexible ducting or section of flue pipe, minimum 25cm (10in) long

30 x 60cm (1 x 2ft) concrete slab roof

For the smoke chamber

old cabinet or wooden frame

1 bundle of cedar shingles (optional)

copper nails (optional)

jigsaw

heatproof silicone sealant

drill (optional)

wine corks (optional)

2–3 wire racks

4–6 wooden batons

screws

temperature probe

For lighting

cold-smoke generator (optional)

sawdust or wood chips

matches and tea-light candle

Cold Smoker

A cold smoker consists of a firebox and a large smoke chamber, connected by a flue. The smoker should be located outside, near enough to the house that you can check on it, but away from windows, doors, and neighbours.

The Method

01 First, make the firebox. For this, you can modify a small wood-burning stove by cementing a flue in place of the chimney. Alternatively, you can make your own from bricks. To do this, mix the cement mortar with a bucket of water, then lay a cement base of 30cm² (1ft²) and embed the fire bricks in it. Allow to dry overnight, then build the walls to create a firebox 30 x 30 x 60cm (1 x 1 x 2ft), with a hole at the front for a door and another in the top for the flue. Set the door frame and door into the hole at the front and add a layer of facing bricks around it. Embed with plenty of mortar. Cement the ducting or flue into the top hole at an upward angle – the firebox needs to sit lower than the smoke chamber, to allow the smoke to draw upwards through the flue. After 24 hours, once the walls have dried solid, taper another layer of bricks on top to form the roof foundation and lay a concrete slab on top to seal it.

02 Next, make the smoke chamber. This should be located 30–50cm (12–20in) from the firebox. Either use an old cabinet or build a wooden frame, but don't use treated wood to avoid chemicals. If building a frame, clad it with cedar shingles (these are lightweight, durable, and good for insulation), affixed with copper nails.

03 Use a jigsaw to cut a hole near the base of the smoke chamber for the flue from the firebox to feed into. This should be elevated above the firebox outlet so that the smoke rises into the smoke chamber. Seal around the gaps with heatproof silicone sealant or mortar.

04 Make an adjustable gap in the roof to allow varied airflow. The simplest method is to leave a gap in the roof shingle and then create a wooden hat that can slide on and off. Alternatively, drill 5–6 holes in the top and plug with wine corks to further adjust the draw.

05 Install 2–3 stainless-steel wire racks in the chamber to allow you to hang fish or lay food for smoking **(fig. a)**. Cut the racks to size, then screw wooden batons into place to create shelves for them to sit on.

06 If your smoke chamber does not already have a door, measure the space and build a frame that fits inside the front face. Attach a door with hinges and secure it shut with a simple latch. Make sure the door is sealed well enough to stop too much smoke escaping. Install a temperature probe (you can find these online) inside the smoke chamber to monitor the heat inside.

07 In the firebox, light a small fire or a cold-smoke generator, which is filled with sawdust and produces a clean, cool smoke for up to 10 hours. Light it with a tea-light candle, which allows the sawdust to catch over a few minutes **(fig. b)**. Once smoking, you are all set – place your food in the smoker, shut the door, and leave to smoke for the required time.

EXPERT TIPS

If you don't have a cold-smoke generator, arrange 2–3 handfuls of sawdust in a coil inside the firebox and light by placing a couple of hot embers on a piece of newspaper, then putting this on the sawdust.

I'm a huge fan of vertical stack smokers like the ProQ, as they are simple to manoeuvre and you can easily check the smoking progress without disturbing the process, using small doors in the sides.

Figure a.

Figure b.

THE PRACTICE

Smoked Cheese

Smoking adds a sweet, woody note to cheese that complements its natural tang and creamy flavour. You can smoke any cheese; hard cheeses take a little longer than soft cheeses, but hard blue cheese tends to smoke more easily than a crumbly or soft Gorgonzola, and Stilton is always a winner. Serve with crackers, melted on a burger, or simply with a glass of port and it will steal the show.

MAKES

500g (1lb 2oz) cheese

INGREDIENTS

500g (1lb 2oz) blue cheese
1 tbsp maple syrup

EQUIPMENT

cold smoker (see pp.190–91)
4 tbsp maple wood chips
tray
ice cubes
baking parchment or beeswax wrap

Method

01 Remove any rind from the cheese, then place it in the freezer for 10–15 minutes. This brings down the temperature of the cheese and dries out the surface slightly, which will help the glaze to adhere and the smoke to penetrate. Next, lightly brush the chilled cheese with the maple syrup glaze **(fig. a)**.

02 Prime a cold smoker (see pp.190–91) using the maple wood chips, then place the cheese in the smoke chamber **(fig. b)**. The optimum temperature range for cold smoking is below 30°C (85°F), so to help keep the temperature as low as possible, place a tray of ice cubes below the cheese. Smoke the cheese for 2–4 hours, turning it every half an hour.

03 When you have finished smoking, open the door of the smoker but leave the cheese inside and allow it to rest for 15 minutes, before wrapping it in baking parchment or beeswax wrap. Place the cheese in the fridge for 2–4 days before enjoying, to allow the flavours to mature. Keep refrigerated and consume within 2 weeks.

EXPERT TIPS

You can cold smoke all sorts of different cheeses and even try other dairy products, such as butter or hard-boiled eggs. Reduce the smoking time slightly for more delicate soft cheeses, to avoid masking their gentle tangy flavour.

———

Don't be tempted to try the cheese before you've given it a couple of days to mature in the fridge. This time is essential, as the cheese may taste slightly bitter until the smoked flavour has been absorbed and had a chance to mellow.

Figure a.

Figure b.

MAKES

400g (14oz) pâté

INGREDIENTS

1 whole mackerel, gutted
25g (scant 1oz) sea salt
25g (scant 1oz) caster sugar
100g (3½oz) crème fraîche
1 tbsp lemon juice
1 tsp horseradish sauce
pinch of cracked black pepper

EQUIPMENT

fish tweezers
cold smoker (see pp.190–91)
4 tbsp oak sawdust
tray
ice cubes

THE PRACTICE

Smoked Mackerel Pâté

Mackerel is my favourite whole smoked fish. This recipe has been in my
family for over 30 years and was one of the first things I ever learnt to cook.
I have very fond memories of days spent with my grandpa, mastering the
art of making chutney and smoked mackerel pâté. It's superb with a spiced
damson chutney and slices of apple.

Method

01 Remove the head and tail of the mackerel, then lay the fish on its side and slice cleanly along the belly **(fig. a)**. Give the fish a rinse in some cold running water, then pat dry with kitchen paper.

02 Press down on the backbone to flatten out the fish, then turn it over so that it is skin-side down and snip the backbone away from the flesh with scissors. Remove any further bones with fish tweezers.

03 Place the butterflied mackerel in a dish and sprinkle with the sea salt and sugar **(fig. b)**, then cover and leave to cure in the fridge for 30 minutes–1 hour.

04 Rinse the fish to remove the cure, pat dry with kitchen paper, then leave on a wire rack in a cool, well-ventilated place to air-dry for 1 hour while preparing the cold smoker.

05 Prime the smoker by tightly packing the oak sawdust in a spiral and allowing a dense smoke to form. Place the fish in the smoker on a wire rack, allowing good air circulation around it and adding a tray of ice underneath to keep the temperature below 30°C (85°F). Smoke for 6–8 hours.

06 Once smoked, make the pâté. Remove the fish skin, break up the smoked mackerel, and combine with the crème fraîche, lemon juice, horseradish sauce, and black pepper. Mash with a fork to a coarse pâté texture **(fig. c)** and serve with crackers or toast. Keep for up to 1 week in the fridge.

EXPERT TIPS

Those less experienced at preparing fish can use ready-filleted mackerel for this recipe. Alternatively, ask your fishmonger to butterfly the fish for you.

Mix 1 teaspoon of crushed peppercorns and 1 teaspoon of grated horseradish root and rub onto the fish to add more warmth to the smoked mackerel flavour.

Figure a.

Figure b.

Figure c.

THE POSSIBILITIES

No Smoke Without Fire

Once you've mastered the basic skills of cold smoking, focus on the various subtle notes of different woods and learn about the delicate craft of playing with fire.

EARTHY AROMAS

Normally meat and fish dominate the limelight for smoked foods, but I'm a massive fan of applying the same process to vegetables.

- Cold-smoked garlic **(fig. a)** can be used in place of fresh garlic in many recipes. Try crushing the cloves into a smoked garlic butter and using on roast chicken, or as a base for a pesto with sage and walnuts.
- Tofu can often be accused of being bland, but if you cold smoke it and then use it in a stir-fry, you can add great depth of flavour.
- Smoked chickpeas are delicious if roasted in a little oil and sprinkled with salt and paprika **(fig. b)**. These crunchy roasted treats make yummy snacks with a cold beer and are fantastic in a tagine or vegetarian curry.
- Smoked hummus is always a real crowd-pleaser. Try smoking butter beans as a replacement for chickpeas in a smoked bean hummus, or use smoked beetroot with apricot and cumin for a colourful alternative.

Try ... Smoked hummus Smoke 250g (9oz) chickpeas drizzled with 1 tablespoon of olive oil over some apple wood chips for 2 hours. Then blitz with 1 tablespoon of tahini, the juice of 1 lemon, 1 smoked garlic clove, a pinch of smoked sea salt, and 1 tablespoon of olive oil.

Figure a.

Figure b.

Figure c.

Figure d.

Figure e.

FIRE AND WATER

Oily fish tends to be better for smoking than more delicate white fish. Try having a go at all sorts of shellfish and even mixing dried seaweed in with your wood chips.

- Cold smoking a whole side of salmon or haddock can be immensely satisfying. Once cured, the fish will take 6–12 hours to smoke.
- Kippers **(fig. c)** are cold-smoked herring and a speciality of northeast England. Try adding to a kedgeree and serving with a poached egg.
- Smoked cod roe is easy to make and so much tastier than shop-bought taramasalata.
- Mussels, cockles, and even oysters are yummy cold smoked. I tend to cook them first and then smoke them over oak for a delicious snack or a garnish for grilled fish.

Try ... Smoked cod roe (fig. d) Cure 300g (10oz) cod roe with 75g (2½oz) sea salt flakes, 1 teaspoon of fennel seeds, and 1 teaspoon of cracked black pepper in the fridge for 2–3 hours, then cold smoke for 4 hours. Peel away the membrane surrounding the roe and then blitz in a food processor with the juice of 1 lemon, 50g (1¾oz) breadcrumbs, a pinch of salt, and a drizzle of olive oil. Serve with warm pitta bread.

SMOKED DELIGHTS

You can try cold smoking almost anything in your kitchen, so give in to adventure. There are very few limits and it's great fun.

- Cold-smoked avocado makes an excellent guacamole with chipotle chilli peppers.
- Smoked pears **(fig. e)** are a traditional Ukrainian snack and are cold smoked several times until they are dried and full of flavour.
- Sea salt flakes or oils can be smoked and then used as extra-flavoursome seasoning.

"

Smoke doesn't have to be reserved just for salmon or bacon. It can be used to bring another layer to delicate ingredients such as cheese curds, flowers, or even ice.

"

> The chemical chain reaction from slow-moving, fractal clouds of sweet wood smoke can transport food into another flavour dimension. Like a low-lying woodland mist, cold smoking radically transforms the foodie landscape.

Project 22
HOT SMOKING

Succulent woody treats beneath a sweet, spicy, caramelized smoked skin.

SKILL LEVEL Medium: fire management takes some skill; basting, marinating, and curing add complexity, but the cooking style is humble.

TIMINGS 30 minutes–12 hours prep; 10 minutes–12 hours smoking.

Hot-smoked brisket
Brisket rubbed with rosemary will cook slowly on a hot smoker while absorbing the flavours of the wood smoke.

THE SCIENCE

Indirect Cooking

Hot smoking is a form of cooking that relies on an indirect heat source, which cooks the food while infusing it with smoky flavour. It can be done at high temperatures for a short time, as with hot-smoked fish, or slowly, at a lower temperature of 110–125°C (230–260°F), for large joints of meat. It's this low, slow process that breaks down the tougher connective tissues in meat, leaving you with a delicious, juicy end result.

LOW AND SLOW

Meats such as ribs, brisket, and pork shoulder, which are full of connective tissue filled with collagen, benefit from low, slow cooking. When cooked fast at a high heat, collagen contracts and becomes tough, but if you smoke meat at a lower temperature for several hours, the collagen breaks down and melts. Water released from the meat mixes with the melting collagen to create gelatine – a kind of meat jelly. This is called rendering and is integral to making meat juicy and flavourful. The process needs heat, but as the cooking has to be slow to prevent drying out, it can't be too intensive and must therefore be indirect. Many hot smokers feature a water pan, which also helps control the heat by providing a buffer between the food and the heat source.

THE SMOKE RING

When wood burns it produces the chemical compound nitric oxide, which dissolves when it hits the surface of meat, losing its oxygen molecules in the process. It then becomes acidic and tries to find something new to connect with in order to stabilize. What it finds in meat is the protein myoglobin; myoglobin attracts the acid and pulls it into the meat, causing smoked food to take on those delicious smoky flavours. This reaction also produces a stable pink protein, which forms a beautiful ring around the outer millimetres of the meat, known as the "smoke ring". It takes several hours for the smoke ring to form. It is therefore regarded among BBQ enthusiasts as the mark of real smoky flavour – the result of lots of time and effort.

Smoke reactions
The nitric oxide in smoke reacts with the myoglobin in meat, causing the smoky flavour to penetrate the meat and a pink "smoke ring" to form.

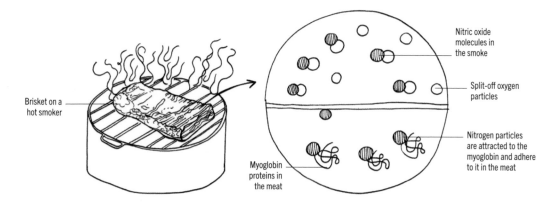

Brisket on a hot smoker

Nitric oxide molecules in the smoke

Split-off oxygen particles

Nitrogen particles are attracted to the myoglobin and adhere to it in the meat

Myoglobin proteins in the meat

THE PRACTICE

Set Up a Hot Smoker

Confidence and practice are key to managing your heat source when hot smoking food. It is important to get involved with the wood and coals – don't keep your distance and think that the fire will look after itself. Fire cooking is a living process that requires small adjustments. Your tongs will become an extension of your arm for keeping the temperatures constant and the heat steady.

Figure a.

Figure b.

Figure c.

EQUIPMENT

kettle or drum BBQ, or hot smoker
   with grill rack (see Expert Tips,
   right)
chimney starter (see Expert Tips,
   right)
kindling
natural firelighter
charcoal
blowtorch
long-handled tongs
heatproof gloves or welding
   gauntlets
tray
2 handfuls of wood chips, such as
   oak, hickory, apple, or maple

Method

01   First, light the hot smoker. Fill a chimney starter with a few pieces of kindling, natural firelighter, and charcoal. Use a blowtorch to light the charcoal from underneath **(fig. a)** and allow to burn for 20–30 minutes. If you don't have a chimney starter, form a stack using the firelighters, kindling, and some charcoal in the hot smoker and light it.

02   Once your charcoal embers are glowing hot, pour them from the chimney starter into the hot smoker **(fig. b)**, then spread them out and push them to one side of the smoker using long-handled tongs. Wear heatproof gloves or welding gauntlets as you do this.

03   Take a handful of wood chips **(fig. c)** and throw them directly onto the hot coals. Secure the lid of your smoker and wait for 3–5 minutes until the wood chips start to smoke, then place the food on the grill. Place a tray on another grill rack underneath the food and above the coals to protect it from the direct heat. This tray can either catch fat drips as the food renders or it can be filled with iced water, which will help lower the temperature for longer hot-smoked recipes.

04   Smoke until the food is cooked – the timing will vary depending on your ingredients. Hot-smoked fish and vegetables will take less time than large joints of meat. When hot smoking for low and slow recipes, you will need to top up the fire with more lit charcoal and another handful of wood chips.

EXPERT TIPS

A kettle BBQ or vertical stack smoker like the ProQ is an excellent way to start and they can be used for many of the methods in this section. Also consider a ceramic hot smoker like a Big Green Egg or Kamado Joe. You can structure all of these with hot coals on one side and a tray to protect your food from direct heat on the other.

———

A chimney starter is a section of flue pipe with a handle and a grill inside to suspend charcoal and light it efficiently. It's an invaluable piece of kit to get you hot smoking. It makes it easier to pour lit charcoal into your smoker and top up the smoker every hour or two.

———

Stove-top smokers are portable, easy to assemble, easy to clean, and you can make a small batch of smoked mackerel or salmon, without firing up your larger smokers or BBQ. You can even improvise using a lidded roasting tray with a wire rack inside.

THE PRACTICE

Smoked Brisket

With its rich infusion of hickory wood, this iconic dish doffs its cap to the Deep South BBQ. The longer you can set aside to smoke your brisket, the deeper the smoky layer of flavour and the more succulent the meat. My recipe uses a transatlantic combination of spices and herbs that complements the lightly smoked beef, especially when served with slaw and sour pickles.

MAKES

2kg (4½lb) smoked brisket

INGREDIENTS

2kg (4½lb) beef brisket
For the rub
2 tbsp chopped rosemary, plus
    extra for sprinkling
1 tbsp cracked black peppercorns
1 tbsp sea salt
1 tbsp paprika
1 tsp brown sugar
1 tsp ground coffee
1 tsp chilli powder
1 tsp garlic powder
1 tsp grated horseradish

EQUIPMENT

spice grinder, food processor, or
    pestle and mortar
charcoal
hot smoker (see pp.202–03)
tray
2 handfuls of hickory chips
meat probe
6 bourbon barrel chunks

Method

01 First, make the spice rub. Blitz all your herbs and spices in a spice grinder or food processor, or crush in a pestle and mortar, then rub the mixture all over the brisket and leave for 1 hour **(fig. a)**.

02 Light the charcoal in the hot smoker 30–45 minutes ahead of when you plan to start cooking and keep the temperature relatively low – as close to 110°C (230°F) as you can. Place a tray filled with water under a grill away from the hot coals – this will keep the brisket moist during cooking. Sprinkle the brisket with extra rosemary and place fat-side up on the grill and over the tray **(fig. b)**.

03 Add 1 handful of the hickory chips to the fire and smoke for 5–8 hours, depending on the time you have available (the longer the better), checking the temperature of the brisket regularly with a meat probe. Aim for 90°C (190°F) inside the meat. The temperature in the smoker should be around 120°C (250°F) (most smokers have their own built-in thermometer). Add more lit charcoal if you need to boost the fire during such a long cooking time. Halfway through cooking, add the second handful of hickory chips and the bourbon barrel chunks for a steady, light smoke and to add sweet oak tones and caramel notes to the flavour.

04 Once smoked, rest your brisket for at least 1 hour in a warm place, then slice thickly and serve.

EXPERT TIPS

There is a Texan cheat that can be employed, which is to wrap the brisket in foil for the last hour of smoking. This is a little pit master's secret that traps steam and meat juices in the foil, tenderizing the meat even further.

———

If creating your own rub, keep it simple – don't use everything in your spice rack. You can get away with just salt, pepper, and cayenne. If time allows, rub your brisket the night before you intend to smoke it.

———

Try making a sweetened BBQ "mop" with sugar or syrup, vinegar or cider, and plenty of warming spices to brush onto the brisket partway through cooking. This will make for an even moister brisket and more caramelized crust.

———

If cooking a different-sized cut, a good rule is to cook brisket for 1 hour 15 minutes for every 500g (1lb 2oz) at 120°C (250°F).

Figure a.

Figure b.

MAKES

1 smoked trout or salmon

INGREDIENTS

1 whole 750g (1lb 10oz) sea trout
    or salmon, gutted
handful of fresh herbs, such as dill,
    parsley, chives
6 lemon slices
1 tsp fennel seeds
1 tsp dried rose petals
zest of 1 lemon or orange
salt and pepper
For the brine
2 tbsp salt
2 tsp sugar
500ml (16fl oz) water

EQUIPMENT

non-reactive brining container
cedar plank
charcoal
kindling
kettle or drum BBQ or hot smoker
    (see pp.202–03)
2 handfuls of hickory wood chips

THE PRACTICE

Plank-smoked Cedar Trout

Smoking fish on a wooden plank solves the age-old problem of delicate fish
falling through the grates and feeding the BBQ gods. You can buy planks of
various woods, and each will impart different flavours; cedar, used here, brings
a hearty forest taste and works especially well with sea trout or salmon. Serve
with beetroot, horseradish, crème fraîche, samphire, and fermented red kraut.

Method

01 First, make the brine. In a pan, warm the salt and sugar in the water until dissolved, allow to cool, then place the whole fish in a brining container and cover with the cure. Make sure the fish is completely submerged, weighing it down if necessary so it doesn't float. Seal the container and place in the fridge to cure for at least 2 hours.

02 Before smoking, soak the cedar plank in water for at least 30 minutes – this will keep the fish moist during cooking and prevent the plank from burning in your BBQ or hot smoker. You could also soak it in fruit juice or cider for extra-special flavour.

03 Light the charcoal and kindling in the BBQ or hot smoker and get it up to a good temperature, at least 70–80°C (160–175°F), then add the hickory wood chips just before you start cooking. When they start to smoke over the hot coals you are ready to cook your fish. This process should take about 30–45 minutes. You want the grill to reach 180°C (350°F).

04 Remove the lightly cured trout from the brine and pat dry with kitchen paper. Place the herbs and lemon slices on the soaked plank **(fig. a)**, then lay the trout on top. Season the fish with salt and pepper to taste, then mix the fennel seeds, rose petals, and lemon or orange zest, and stuff the belly cavity with the mixture. Allow to rest at room temperature for half an hour to dry out. If you are placing your plank at an angle, tack the fish to the plank with a nail to hold it in place.

05 When the grill has reached the right temperature, place the plank on the grill and hot smoke the fish for 20 minutes until the skin is golden and the flesh flaky **(fig. b)**. Insert a fork into the centre of the fish for 5–10 seconds to check if it is cooked through. If the metal feels hot to the touch when you pull it out, the fish is done. Serve immediately.

EXPERT TIPS

Wooden grilling planks are normally thin pieces of wood, about 15 x 30cm (6 x 12in) in size. They can be used a few times, but I tend to use them once and then break them up for kindling, as the resins produced during burning can taint the flavour of the food. You can get planks in different sizes and with a fine, medium, or rough grain – the rougher the grain, the more smoke will circulate off the plank's surface.

———

The risk when smoking food is that it can dry out while cooking. Plank smoking using soaked wood, however, keeps your food moist, as the food is in contact with wet, cold wood rather than the hot grill itself.

———

Any food that you might smoke — meat, veg, or fruit – can be cooked on a plank, though I mainly use this method for fish and aubergines, which particularly benefit.

Figure a.

Figure b.

THE POSSIBILITIES

Some Like It Hot

Hot smoking boldly celebrates your star ingredient, whether it's chicken, shellfish, or oily fish. Have fun playing with aromatics and wood chips for more complex smoke profiles.

FINGER-LICKIN' CHICKEN

Chicken absorbs smoked flavour like a sponge, so it's the perfect testing ground for flavours from different woods and good BBQ rubs.

- Smoked chicken will take a Sunday roast to the next level **(fig. a)**. Make a simple BBQ spiced rub and cook the whole bird for 1–2 hours in a hot smoker until tender and juicy.

- Try adding aromatics, herb pesto, and lemon under the skin of chicken breasts to keep them moist during smoking.
- For a Caribbean smokehouse recipe, rub a whole chicken with smoky jerk spices, then place an open can of beer inside the cavity while it smokes for 1–2 hours. The beer evaporates, marinating the bird as it smokes.

Try ... Hot-smoked chicken breast (fig. b)
Stuff two 200g (7oz) chicken breasts with 1 teaspoon of finely chopped garlic, 1 teaspoon of chopped tarragon, 1 teaspoon of chopped parsley, and 1 teaspoon of chopped chives, plus the zest of 1 lemon. Drizzle both breasts with 1 tablespoon of olive oil and place on a wire rack in a hot smoker at 180°C (350°F). Smoke over cherry wood chips for 20 minutes or until cooked through. Serve with a fresh green salad.

Figure a.

Figure b.

Figure c.

Figure d.

My favourite aspect of hot smoking is the flexibility and freedom it provides. You can add a whole host of aromatics to your heat source and reap the rewards from their distinctive aromas.

PLENTY MORE FISH IN THE SEA

Hot-smoked fish is quick and easy and can pack a serious punch of smoky flavour.

- Try hot smoking mussels, clams, and cockles in their shells at 180°C (355°F) over apple or oak chips for 10 minutes. Serve with samphire and a zingy chilli and coriander salsa.
- Mackerel is delicious served with chimichurri salsa, green apple, and charred lemon, on a bed of shredded Little Gem lettuce **(fig. c)**.
- Hot-smoked salmon **(fig. d)** works well served on crumpets or with some cooling sauce and refreshing pickles.

Try … Hot-smoked salmon crumpets Sprinkle 2 tablespoons of apple wood chips into the base of a stove-top hot smoker, ensuring even coverage. Season 450g (1lb) skinned salmon fillets with 1 teaspoon of seaweed salt. Seal the smoker, then place on a gas hob or fire. As soon as smoke has begun to form, place the salmon fillets on the wire rack inside the smoker and cook over a high heat for 5–7 minutes, until the salmon is an opaque pink throughout. Serve flaked with horseradish and crème fraîche on a toasted crumpet.

AROMATIC INFUSIONS

Tea leaves, herbs and spices, citrus peel, and wood all add their signature scent to smoke.

- Try Earl Grey with trout, jasmine and lapsang souchong with beetroot, duck, or plums, and camomile with a delicate fillet of bass.
- All woods have different aromas and tastes. Oak is excellent for robust oily fish and rich meats, cherry is sweeter and works well with duck breast, while apple is a great all-rounder.
- Dried thyme, rosemary, liquorice, and cinnamon bark all have a distinctive scent. Smoking goat's cheese or mushrooms with herbs instead of wood gives a great aroma.

OUTDOOR
COOKING

———

Project 23
CAMPFIRE COOKING
Slowing down, learning from the outdoor kitchen, and working with fire.

SKILL LEVEL Medium: fire can be managed but never fully controlled.

TIMINGS 30 minutes for lighting; 30 minutes for flames; ember plateau 30–40 minutes; residual heat 1 hour.

Dirty beets and onions
Cooking over the glowing embers of an outdoor fire is visceral and instinctive.

THE SCIENCE

Combustion

Fire is the result of a chemical reaction known as combustion, in which fuel, when heated, reacts with oxygen to create rapid oxidation, resulting in heat, light, and other by-products. I have always been fascinated by this process. Lighting a BBQ, stoking the embers, sitting around a campfire, or digging an underground oven rekindles a connection with food and with each other, and offers delicious escapism from the indoor kitchen.

FIRE LIFE CYCLE

Every fire starts with ignition. As lit wood is heated up by flaring yellow flames of 100–200°C (210–390°F), the water in the wood starts to boil and then evaporate. The white smoke that this produces (a mixture of soot particles, droplets of liquid, and chemical gases) will continue until the moisture is gone, volatile gases start to be released, and the heat has built sufficiently to fully combust in an exothermic reaction. This gasification of wood is sometimes called the flashover. With temperatures rising from 200–600°C (390–1110°F), this ferocious time in a fire's life cycle may be good for flash-grilling steaks but it doesn't last long; embers provide a longer, more constant temperature ideal for cooking.

EMBERS

Once the flames die down, you are left with glowing embers. These can vary in temperature, but when they glow bright orange, almost white, the exothermic reaction results in maximum heat production and temperatures of 1200–1600°C (2190–2910°F). Eventually the temperature plateaus, and once the embers have broken down you are left with a white ash of potassium, calcium, and uncombusted carbon cinders, which has a gentle residual heat. You can cook some ingredients slowly in these ashes – vegetables such as onions, potatoes, or beetroots work well – but the optimum cooking time is when the hot flames are replaced with intense embers, which provide a long-lasting, clean heat.

Wood combustion
The cellulose in wood rapidly oxidizes when it burns, producing energy in the form of heat and light, as well as carbon dioxide and water vapour.

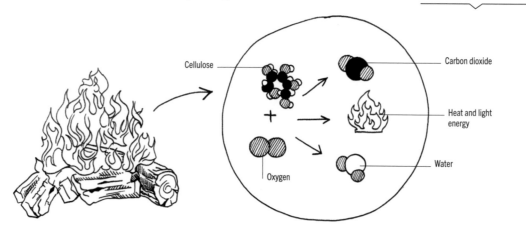

Cellulose

Oxygen

Carbon dioxide

Heat and light energy

Water

THE PRACTICE

Make a Fire for Cooking

The simple pleasures of building a fire and cooking outdoors are intoxicating. Making the jump from your indoor kitchen to wild cooking requires learning new skills to tame and control your fire. Enjoy it – there's nothing more sociable than cooking and eating around a fire.

EQUIPMENT

few handfuls of tinder
few handfuls of kindling
matches
blowpipe (optional)
heatproof gloves
10 seasoned logs, plus extra if
    needed (see Expert Tips,
    opposite)
grill grate
shovel or long-handled grill hoe
long-handled tongs
charcoal (optional)
chimney starter (optional)

Figure a.

Method

01 Arrange a small pile of tinder and kindling in a wigwam shape. A collection of dried leaves, pine cones, grasses, and twigs works well as tinder – the drier your ingredients, the faster your fire will light.

02 Ignite the tinder with a match and watch as the structure catches, adding more tinder if necessary **(fig. a)**. Blow into the fire using a blowpipe if you need to aid combustion with more air **(fig. b)**.

03 Next, wearing heatproof gloves, place 2 dry logs parallel to each other either side of the fire, approximately 30cm (12in) apart, then bridge across them with 2 more logs to protect your fire from wind. Lay some more kindling in the gap to bridge the hollow in the middle, then build up 4 more logs, alternating across in the same square formation. Layer more kindling in the hollow, then, maintaining the same open structure, add 2 more logs to complete the tower **(fig. c)**.

04 Once the fire has taken, allow plenty of time – up to 45 minutes – for the flames to establish and the fire to mature before it burns down to embers.

05 Next, spread out the burning wood into an even layer. Rake the glowing orange embers underneath a grill grate with a shovel or long-handled grill hoe. You want an even bed of embers for cooking, but not a shallow one. The deeper the bed, the higher the heat. Use long-handled tongs to make little adjustments here and there to fill any gaps in the bed.

06 Rather than adding more wood to intense embers, I like to start off some charcoal in a chimney starter and use that to top up the wood embers. Charcoal can be a useful addition for a longer, more even burn. That said, extra logs will also work and can be started off to one side, repeating the process of making another log stack and spreading the embers over the existing fire.

07 Use your hand to gauge the temperature of your embers by holding it 30cm (12in) above the fire. You should be able to feel hotter and cooler spots, indicating where you need to adjust the coals and embers with tongs to fill in those cooler gaps and top up if required to create an even heat source. Once this has been achieved, the fire is ready for cooking.

EXPERT TIPS

Don't use treated woods or firelighters for cooking, as the toxic chemicals can taint your food.

———

Always use seasoned hardwoods (woods that have been left for a few seasons to dry out) like oak, alder, or hickory; these are drier than green wood and burn much better.

———

Wood burns faster than charcoal. If using wood alone, be prepared to replenish the embers every 20 to 30 minutes. Replenishing with charcoal will keep the fire going for longer at a more constant temperature.

———

Keep a fire extinguisher, water, or sand nearby as a precaution, and extinguish the fire once finished.

Figure b.

Figure c.

INGREDIENTS

4 beetroots

2 red onions

For the salad

2 tbsp whole walnuts

100g (3½oz) feta-style cheese, crumbled (see pp.114–15)

4 caper berries

1 orange, zested and segmented

1 tsp chopped dill

drizzle of olive oil

pinch of sea salt flakes

For the dip

2 tbsp yogurt

1 tsp harissa

EQUIPMENT

campfire (see pp.214–15)

heatproof gloves

long-handled tongs

THE PRACTICE

Dirty Cooking

Once you've tried cooking "dirty" directly on the hot embers of a campfire, you won't look back. Dirty cooking can be fast and intense, but by zoning your fire pit into areas for direct or indirect cooking, you can also take it slow and gentle. You can roast whole vegetables or steaks straight on the glowing embers – just brush off the ash and peel blackened skins off vegetables before serving.

DIRTY BEETS SALAD

The balance of sweetness and woody char in the beetroots works fantastically with orange and creamy feta, while the dirty onions are a revelation, packed with caramelized sweetness. Peel the cooked beetroot with a spoon and discard the skin before serving.

Method

01 Build and light your campfire as on pp.214–15. Once you have an even heat, put on heatproof gloves and roast the beetroots and onions in their skins directly on the bed of hot embers. Cook for 40–45 minutes, turning periodically with some long-handled tongs until blackened on all sides and tender in the middle.

02 Allow to cool on a chopping board for 5–10 minutes, then carefully remove the onion skins and beetroot peel. Next, quarter the beets and slice the caramelized red onions into segments.

03 Toss the dirty beets and onions in a rustic salad of walnuts, crumbled feta-style cheese (see pp.114–15), caper berries, and orange segments **(fig. a)**. Garnish the salad with the orange zest and chopped dill, then drizzle with the olive oil and season with a pinch of sea salt flakes. Finally, to make the dip, whisk together the yogurt and harissa with a fork, then serve in a dipping bowl with the salad.

ALSO TRY

Dirty leeks (fig. b) To make dirty leeks, simply place the leeks whole in the embers and cook for 20–30 minutes. Turn periodically with tongs and serve shredded with melted butter for a sweet and smoky side dish.

Dirty scallops with seaweed and Prosecco (fig. c) This is one of my favourite dirty recipes. Add 50g (1¾oz) seaweed butter to 6 scallops in their shells and place directly onto hot embers. Cook for 2–3 minutes. Halfway through cooking, when piping hot, spritz with 75ml (2½fl oz) Prosecco or sparkling wine, then, using tongs, turn the scallops to sear them on both sides. Once cooked, garnish with chopped flat-leaf parsley and lemon juice to serve.

EXPERT TIPS

Try covering food with a layer of hot embers to bury it. This removes the need to turn the produce and is great for robust root veg.

Add whole sprigs of fresh herbs to the coals as an aromatic layer to cook meat, fish, and vegetables on. This will slightly dampen the fierce heat but also add more flavour.

Figure a.

Figure b.

Figure c.

THE PRACTICE

Grilling

Grilling meat, fish, and vegetables quickly on a rack set over an intense heat source locks in flavour. Delicate items like fish benefit from being grilled on a protective bed of lemon and herbs (such as rosemary or thyme sprigs) to infuse flavour and stop them sticking or falling through the grates. You can also take grilling to the next level by basting with marinades or glazes for added moisture.

SERVES 4

INGREDIENTS

1kg (2¼lb) king prawns
1 tbsp chilli oil
1 tsp smoked salt
For the marinade
150ml (5fl oz) red wine
6 sprigs of thyme
2 tbsp honey
1 tbsp sweet paprika
1 bulb of garlic cloves, peeled
    and thinly sliced
1 tbsp chopped dill
1 tbsp finely sliced green chilli

EQUIPMENT

campfire with grill rack (see
    pp.214–15), charcoal grill,
    or BBQ
skewers (metal, or wooden,
    soaked beforehand)
basting brush
long-handled tongs

Figure a.

KING PRAWN SKEWERS

This recipe for chargrilled king prawns is a corker. The paprika, red wine, and honey all add sweetness, while the aromatic thyme and garlic infuse through the fierce heat. This method toasts the prawns in their shells, providing the perfect finger-licking BBQ starter.

Method

01 Prepare your grill 30 minutes before cooking and wait for the embers to reach an intense heat.

02 Combine all the marinade ingredients in a cast-iron or copper saucepan and place on the grill to warm. Heat for 5 minutes until the red wine starts to reduce.

03 Feed your prawns onto skewers and drizzle them with a little chilli oil. Season with smoked salt, then spoon or brush on the marinade and place directly on the grill. Cook on one side for 3–4 minutes, basting the prawns with more marinade every minute or two to build up the layers of flavour **(main image)**.

04 Turn the prawns using tongs and grill the other side for another 3–4 minutes, continuing to baste, until the shells are shiny and covered with a generous layer of sticky sauce.

05 Serve with a slice of charred lemon and some focaccia (see pp.128–29) to dip in what remains of the sticky marinade sauce.

ALSO TRY

Herb-stuffed sea bass (fig. a). Stuff two 400g (14oz) line-caught sea bass with a combination of 1 tablespoon of chopped flat-leaf parsley, 1 tablespoon of chopped thyme, 1 tablespoon of sea salt, and the zest of 1 whole lemon. Score the fish skins and rub any excess herbs and zest into the grooves. Tie some butcher's twine around each fish to keep the herbs and lemon in the cavity and brush with 1 tablespoon of olive oil. Place in a grill basket and cook over hot embers for 4–5 minutes on each side until the skin is crisp. Serve with grilled peas in the pod, thinly sliced charred fennel, and a crisp white wine.

Hispi cabbage (fig. b). This is my favourite vegetable on the grill along with the iconic corn on the cob. Melt 100g (3½oz) salted butter, then add in 1 tablespoon of chopped rosemary. Slice 2 hispi cabbages lengthways into quarters, season with 1 teaspoon of sea salt flakes and 1 teaspoon of orange zest, then grill over hot coals for 10 minutes. Baste generously with the rosemary butter while grilling, until the hearts are tender and the external leaves are charred. Serve with sausages and cracked black pepper.

Surf 'n' turf (fig. c). Try grilling scallops with chorizo or steak with langoustine and chimichurri butter; the charred undertones add a meaty quality to shellfish. Add flavoured butter, herbs, and lemon zest to prime the meat for a sweet side, such as grilled tomatoes and onions.

Figure b.

Figure c.

EXPERT TIPS

Grilling indirectly, with the produce set to one side of your heat source, will avoid flare-ups. If meaty juices drip on the fire, the fat can burn and produce dirty smoke that taints the sweeter wood-smoked flavours.

For best results, always start with a clean grill and wait until the coals have reached an intense heat to prevent food sticking to the grill.

THE PRACTICE

Pots and Cans

Fire cookery using pots and cans works via conduction rather than radiation or convection. You can use a cast-iron skillet on a tripod as a buffer from the direct heat, or even hang old tin cans over the embers if you want. Cooking in pots avoids flare-ups from fat dripping onto the coals and bursting into flames, which chars your meat, and can allow for slower cooking and greater control.

Figure a.

Figure b.

Figure c.

SERVES 2

INGREDIENTS

1 tbsp olive oil

2 shallots, finely diced

1 tbsp smoked paprika

1 tsp cracked black pepper

pinch of sea salt flakes

400g (14oz) pinto or haricot beans,
   cooked and drained

2 tbsp tomato purée

1 tbsp molasses

1 tsp finely chopped coriander

1 tsp dried thyme

1 tsp Dijon mustard

50ml (2fl oz) bourbon (optional)

100g (3½oz) smoked streaky
   bacon

a few slices of sourdough toast

EQUIPMENT

cast-iron skillet

campfire (see pp.214–15)

tripod or three even-sized rocks

cast-iron frying pan

BILLYCAN BEANS

Every campfire enthusiast has probably cooked beans at some point. My recipe is inspired by a trip to Boston years ago to develop a BBQ smokehouse pop-up restaurant for festivals. I wanted a popular brunch menu that would suit the whole family and beans are tough to beat. The drunken version with bourbon adds a grown-up angle.

Method

01   Heat a little olive oil in a cast-iron skillet over a fire, either on a tripod or elevated on top of three even-sized rocks. Add the shallots, then cook for 4–5 minutes until they have softened. To control the cooking heat, raise or lower the skillet. Alternatively, spread out the embers to reduce the heat intensity.

02   Add in the paprika, black pepper, and salt with the beans and stir well. Then mix in the tomato purée, molasses, herbs, mustard, and a good splash of bourbon (if using).

03   Bring to a simmer and cook for 15–20 minutes, stirring regularly **(fig. a)**. Add a small cup of water if needed to prevent the beans from drying out.

04   While the beans are simmering, add a drizzle of olive oil to a cast-iron frying pan and add the streaky bacon **(fig. b)**. Cook for a few minutes until crisp. When ready, serve the beans **(fig. c)** with the bacon and toast.

EXPERT TIPS

A good cast-iron skillet or frying pan is in my Top 10 of kit that every outdoor kitchen needs. Try to clean it while still warm, then season it by rubbing oil into the surface and baking in the oven at 150°C (300°F) for 1 hour. Alternatively, leave it over hot embers and rub in oil until it's soaked up. You can also invert a skillet over the embers and leave until the heat burns off any residue inside the pan.

————

Cast-iron pans are virtually indestructible. That said, never place a hot cast-iron pan straight into cold water or it can crack.

————

For a twist on billycan beans, try suspending a number of tin cans over the embers and dividing the bean mixture between them. The difficulty with this way of cooking beans is that they are slightly harder to stir, but it's a fun way of presenting them.

THE PRACTICE

Clambake

I dug my first clambake on the island of Jersey several years ago and in my eyes there is no greater type of beach BBQ. It's a sharing feast that takes some effort to set up, but the reward is completely worth it. Don't get too precious about the work involved – it's basically the grown-up version of building sandcastles.

SERVES 5

INGREDIENTS

1kg (2¼lb) whole lobster
6 oysters
1kg (2¼lb) clams
1kg (2¼lb) mussels
5 corn on the cob, husks removed
1kg (2¼lb) whole Pink Fir Apple
    potatoes, or other waxy varieties
    such as Charlotte or Jersey
    Royals

EQUIPMENT

spade
large flat stones
tinder
kindling
8 dry, seasoned hardwood logs
5kg (11lb) foraged seaweed
    (optional, see Expert Tips, right)
small knife or scissors

Figure a.

CORNISH CLAMBAKE

My Cornish clambake involves a quick dive to forage for some seaweed and enough steamed seafood for the whole family. I also like to add crowd-pleasing vegetables to balance the rich shellfish, and the corn and small potatoes used here will steam at the same speed as the clams. This is a way of cooking that gets everyone involved in the process so that the whole family can really enjoy a shared meal.

Method

01 Start by digging a large hole in the beach about 1m x 50cm x 50cm (3ft x 20in x 20in). Ideally, try to locate it below the high tide line so that the clambake washes away after cooking. Collect a number of large flat stones (15–20 should be enough, depending on their size) and arrange them in the base of your hole. Try to cover all gaps and lay a good foundation for your fire.

02 Build a small fire on top of the stones using some tinder and kindling **(fig. a)**, and once it's caught add the dry, seasoned logs to build up a large fire. Wait for 40–45 minutes until the flames have died down and you're left with glowing hot embers.

03 While you're waiting, forage for the seaweed **(fig. b)**. Use a small knife or scissors to harvest it from below the tide line. Do not pull it from the rocks, as this will damage the plant and ecosystem, or use floating seaweed, as this will be dead and decaying. Try to gather enough to build layers of seaweed in the fire pit.

04 Once the embers are intensely hot in the base of the hole, spread them out across the stones to form an even bed of glowing embers, then add a layer of seaweed on top, followed by the largest of the shellfish – the lobster and oysters.

05 Cover with another layer of seaweed, then add the clams and mussels, the corn, and the potatoes on top. You can bake whole fish, sausages, and other vegetables in your clambake, always placing the larger items in the first layer, nearest to the fire where it is hotter. Cover completely with seaweed and then use your spade to cover the whole clambake with sand **(fig. c)**.

06 Enjoy the beach while you wait for 1–2 hours (depending on when you want to eat) for the seafood to cook, then carefully unearth. Enjoy hot and serve with some seaweed butter and crusty bread.

EXPERT TIPS

If you don't live near a beach, you can try a similar technique by digging a pit oven in the ground.

Wrap your food to protect it from dirt or sand. Here, I've used seaweed, but you can use meadow hay, banana leaves for fish or a salt dough crust for a brisket or joint of lamb. You can also add nettles or herbs for extra flavour.

The longer you cook your food in a clambake or pit oven, the more tender it will be. If the surface of the pit feels too warm to touch, add another layer of sand or soil to keep the heat in.

Figure b.

Figure c.

“

I have always been fascinated by fire. Like many chefs, I find the thrill of cooking in the heat of the kitchen addictive and I feel truly alive in those moments of focus, when you challenge yourself to transform food into something magical. At times, I have felt that the experience of being confined to an indoor kitchen lacked something – immediacy, the raw excitement, and evocative aromas.

”

THE POSSIBILITIES

Playing with Fire

I try to retain the excitement of my early years spent around a campfire and to fuse that with a pioneering outlook when working with fire.

BASTE IT

When you grill and roast over a fire, the greatest risk is drying out the food in the intense heat. There are a number of methods to help prevent this, but the simplest is basting.

- In the US there is a strong tradition of basting with a "BBQ mop". This is a combination of beer, vinegar or apple cider, fruit juice, and spices that forms a tasty crust on pork ribs, brisket, and smoked meats.
- Basting with fats and juices can be easily achieved by placing a drip tray beneath the meat. Try adding a whole bulb of garlic and some fresh herbs to the tray to slowly roast them in the dripping fat, then brush the liquid back onto the meat to keep it moist.
- Blueberry BBQ bourbon sauce is a great basting liquor. Simmer blueberries and sieve them to extract the juice, then mix the juice, bourbon, maple syrup, smoked paprika, and a pinch of cinnamon for a sweet, spicy baste.
- Hispi cabbage is fantastic sliced into quarters and brushed with an aromatic rosemary butter with pink peppercorns. Grill slowly and keep basting until the heart is tender and the outer layers are charred and sweet.

Try ... Rosemary butter with pink peppercorns Make a basting brush by tying several sprigs of rosemary to a 50cm (20in) long stick **(fig. a)**. Melt 200g (7oz) butter, then add in 1 teaspoon of pink peppercorns and the zest of 1 orange. Brush onto grilled meats and vegetables with the rosemary brush.

ASH PARCELS

Foil can protect food from the direct heat and intensity of hot embers by providing a barrier from the coals. A sealed parcel will also lock in moisture and intensify the flavours.

Figure a.

Figure b.

- For a gourmet foil parcel, cook a fillet of sea bass with a splash of white wine, a knob of butter, and some seaweed for 5–6 minutes. Serve with lemon juice and a fennel slaw.
- Drizzle sausages with oil, wrap in foil, and bake in the embers for 10 minutes, then finish over the flames for a minute on a fork. Try adding a splash of red wine, thyme, and honey to a parcel of chorizo sausages.
- Spiced stone fruit in a foil parcel is the easiest BBQ dessert I cook. The wrap protects the fruit from the fierce heat of the grill, while all the juices that would otherwise sizzle away, caramelize with the spices and sugar to form a delicious compote.

Try ... Spiced stone fruit (fig. b) Halve and destone 1kg (2¼lb) plums, peaches, and apricots and arrange on a piece of foil. Add a cinnamon stick, 2 star anise, a vanilla pod split lengthways with the seeds scraped out, and add 1 tablespoon of golden caster sugar. Seal the parcel and bake on the hot embers for 4–5 minutes. Serve with a dollop of clotted cream.

IN THE FRAME

I learnt to cook butterflied fish skewered on a frame of sticks and set over a campfire with my father when I was younger. The fish cooks while the frame supports the delicate flesh **(fig. c)**.

Figure c.

- Try smoking butterflied trout in a frame over oak or apple wood. Serve with an adobo sauce, chimichurri, or a salsa verde.
- The larger version of this type of cooking is based on Argentine BBQ techniques, or *asado*, where an entire lamb or goat carcass is splayed out on metal crosses to receive even heat across a wider surface area.

For most cooks, the campfire is their introduction to an outdoor kitchen. The simple techniques you learn when cooking a fried breakfast on a chilly morning stay with you for ever and are memories to be treasured.

THE POSSIBILITIES

Pots, Pans, and Planks

If you have an idea, chances are there's a rustic device to meet your needs. I've travelled the world and cooked with myriad stoves and grills that never cease to amaze me.

KOTLICHS

This traditional Hungarian-style cooking pot is suspended over the fire by a tripod **(fig. a)**. The contents can easily be stirred and turned for even cooking – perfect for soups and stews.

- Goulash is the iconic kotlich recipe, and a slow-cooked beef or venison version with plenty of sweet paprika is hard to beat.
- A hearty stew in a kotlich makes a great one-pot meal. Try pheasant or rabbit with leeks, carrots, cider, and pearl barley.
- Beer clam chowder is a twist on a classic, using a hoppy IPA. This is perfect beach food, as the recipe tastes best with a blast of sea air.

Try ... Beer clam chowder (fig. b) Soften 2 sticks of sliced celery, ½ bulb of chopped fennel, and 2 diced potatoes over the fire in a kotlich with 50g (1¾oz) butter and 1 tablespoon of olive oil. Add 2 tablespoons of sweetcorn kernels and cook for 5–10 minutes. Next, add 400g (14oz) of diced haddock fillet and 330ml (11fl oz) IPA beer. Rinse and drain 350g (12oz) clams to remove any grit, then add to the pot. Cook for 5 minutes, then add 500ml (16fl oz) double cream. Bring to the boil and finish the chowder with a handful of foraged sea vegetables, such as sea beet and samphire, and 1 tablespoon of coriander. Cook for 1–2 minutes more, season, and serve with bread and butter.

Figure a.

Figure b.

Figure c.

Figure d.

DUTCH OVENS

A Dutch oven is a great way to try your hand at
wild baking. The principles involve placing the
thick-walled cast-iron pot onto hot embers and
covering the lid with more coals so that it cooks
evenly from all angles **(fig. c)**.

- A casserole is a good place to start. Combine
  carrots, leeks, and potatoes with cuts such as
  lamb breast, scrag-end, or neck, then add
  either wine, beer, stock, or chopped tomatoes
  and cook slowly for 2–3 hours.
- Cooking bread in a Dutch oven works
  extremely well – try a sage flatbread **(fig. d)**,
  focaccia, or soda bread. Make sure the pot is
  well seasoned (i.e. warmed at 150°C/300°F
  for 1–2 hours and rubbed with oil
  beforehand) so that the bread doesn't stick.
- Have a go at something sweet in a Dutch
  oven. I love a good winter berry cobbler,
  spiced apple crumble with cinnamon and
  ginger, or a salted caramel apple tarte Tatin.

PLANKS

I often use planks to cook fillets of fish around
the edges of a fire pit (see pp. 206–07). Soak
cedar or alder planks in water first and nail
some aromatics under the fish for more flavour.

- Trout and salmon fillets are both fantastic
  cooked on a plank set around your fire **(fig. e)**
  (see pp.206–07). They smoke slightly and
  absorb the woody aromas but remain moist.
- Food that's difficult to grill can work well on a
  plank. Try soft fruit like mango and bananas
  seasoned with smoked sugar. Softer vegetables
  like tomatoes or aubergines will slow-roast for
  a fantastic salsa or baba ganoush.

Figure e.

Project 24
SPIT ROASTING
Roasted meat turned slowly over fire until cooked to perfection.

SKILL LEVEL Easy: rigging up the spit roast is the most challenging part.

TIMINGS 30 minutes prep and loading up the spit; 4–8 hours cooking.

Shawarma kebab
Spit-roasted lamb, with quinoa tabbouleh, hummus, pickles, and flatbread.

Rotisserie

Spit roasting is slow-cooking at its best. As the spit rotates, heat radiates from the open fire beneath and cooks all sides of the meat evenly. The outside caramelizes with intense flavour from the direct heat, and the inside cooks slowly at a lower temperature, which helps to retain moisture. The juices and melted fats baste the meat as it cooks, intensifying the flavours and keeping the meat succulent. The process may be slow, but it's worth it.

THE MAILLARD REACTION

The Maillard reaction is the process that browns protein-rich meats when they reach 140°C (285°F), creating wonderful flavours. The amino acids in the protein react with the simple sugar molecules in meat, known as reducing sugars, and create new substances, including melanoidins, which are richly aromatic and brown in colour. As the temperature increases, more reactions take place: at 150°C (300°F) twice as many flavour molecules are released as at 140°C (285°F); at 160°C (320°F) the molecular changes peak and you will taste caramel, nutty, and meaty flavours. After this point, however, acrid carcinogens are produced by pyrolysis, or burning, so slow-cooking at below 160°C (320°F) is best when spit roasting.

LOW, SLOW, AND EVEN

Correctly used, an outdoor spit roaster will cook meat at a temperature range of 140–160°C (285–320°F). This is the ideal heat for forming a crispy skin due to the caramelization of the sugars and fats in the meat. The internal temperature of the meat, however, will be significantly lower, tending to remain closer to the optimum level of 68°C (155°F) – the magic number at which collagen breaks down into gelatine (see p.145). As the crust forms on the surface of the food via the Maillard reaction, it forms a protective barrier that locks in moisture, preventing it from evaporating during cooking. The dehydrated crust is full of flavour, but it's also the natural foil that insulates the meat and allows it to cook low and slow until tender.

Maillard reaction
At 140°C (285°F), the proteins react with the sugars in meat, creating new flavour compounds and a tasty brown outer crust. As this crust forms on the surface of the meat, it seals in the juices.

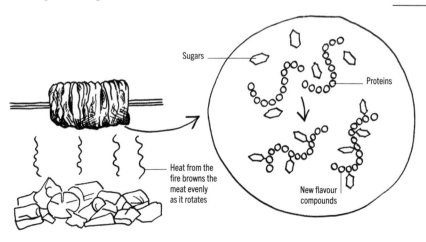

Sugars

Proteins

Heat from the fire browns the meat evenly as it rotates

New flavour compounds

THE PRACTICE

Set Up a Spit Roaster

Setting up a spit roaster is supremely satisfying. No matter what the size, the basic principle remains the same. You need a heat source, a spit suspended over it, and a means to rotate it. Your heat source can either be in a BBQ oven or you can opt for an open fire. The key is to remain attentive – unless, of course, you have a mechanized rotisserie gadget.

EQUIPMENT

spit
BBQ oven or fire pit
roasting tray
grill
chimney starter
handful of kindling
12 seasoned logs
thermometer (optional)
charcoal (optional)
wire
spikes and skewers (optional)

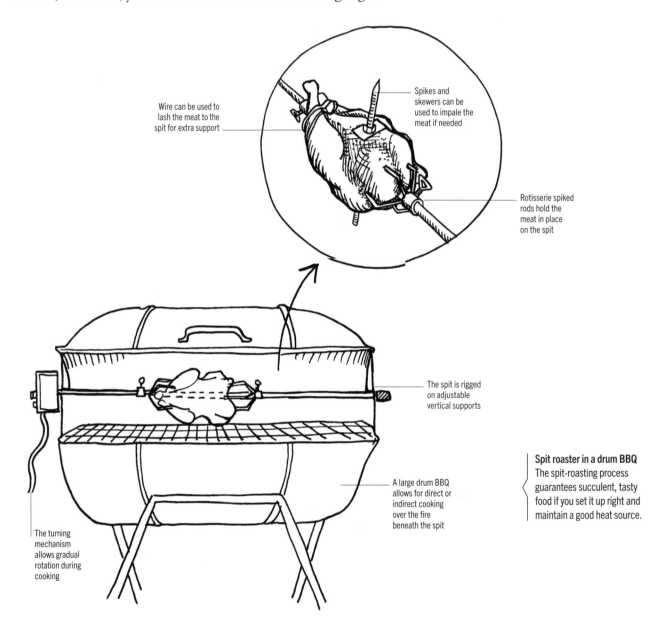

Wire can be used to lash the meat to the spit for extra support

Spikes and skewers can be used to impale the meat if needed

Rotisserie spiked rods hold the meat in place on the spit

The spit is rigged on adjustable vertical supports

A large drum BBQ allows for direct or indirect cooking over the fire beneath the spit

The turning mechanism allows gradual rotation during cooking

Spit roaster in a drum BBQ
The spit-roasting process guarantees succulent, tasty food if you set it up right and maintain a good heat source.

The Method

01 The spit itself needs to be a length of steel at least 1m (3¼ft) in length, sharpened at one end, with vertical supports at each end, which are notched for adjustable height, and a turning mechanism. You can either buy these ready-made or construct your own.

02 Rig up the spit either in a drum BBQ or over an open fire pit, so that it is approximately 30cm (12in) from the direct heat source. Making the spit higher or lower can help control the cooking time. For example, doubling the distance of the food from the hot embers reduces the heat level striking the food by one-third, making for a slower, longer roast.

03 If your BBQ is large enough, offset the spit to one end and add in a roasting tray on a grill beneath the rotisserie so that you can also cook over indirect heat if you wish. If you are spit-roasting a very large item of food, you may not have the option to do this.

04 Using a chimney starter, light your fire with kindling and seasoned logs **(fig. a)**, then wait for 45 minutes for it to burn down to hot embers. Ideally the temperature should be below 160°C (320°F) for cooking meat on a spit roast. If you need to, top up the fire with charcoal lit in the chimney starter to give yourself better control of the temperature. A deep layer of embers will help maintain an even temperature (see pp.214–15).

05 Next, skewer the food onto the spit **(fig. b)**. Position the food centrally for balance and to avoid pressure on the turning mechanism or vertical supports. Use wire to secure the food to the spit so that it stays intact while cooking. To support larger items, I often impale the food with lateral spikes and additional skewers, then lash it onto the main spit with wire.

06 When the fire is ready for cooking, position the spit on the vertical supports at your chosen height over the embers and rotate by a quarter-turn regularly during cooking **(fig. c)**. In general, rotate a larger animal more frequently at first, every 10 minutes, so that a crust forms, then reduce the rate of rotation to every 20–30 minutes to minimize dripping. This allows the juice to stay on the food and maximize flavour.

EXPERT TIPS

I also use a vertical stack BBQ with an automated rotisserie that works fantastically for smaller doner-style kebabs, chickens, and vegetables.

———

You can make your own rig for a whole fish using whittled sticks. Tie the fish onto a stick with string, and add skewers and small side braces if needed to support the flesh. Or, use a fish basket and turn regularly to prevent the flesh falling into the fire.

Figure a.

Figure b.

Figure c.

MAKES

8 kebabs

INGREDIENTS

2kg (4½lb) lamb shoulder, boned
drizzle of olive oil
salt and pepper
For the marinade
20 mint leaves
6 garlic cloves, sliced
2 tbsp chopped dill
1 tbsp ras el hanout
1 tsp smoked chilli flakes
1 tsp smoked sea salt
2 tbsp olive oil
To serve
4 Little Gem lettuces
8 flatbreads, grilled
100ml (3½fl oz) natural yogurt

EQUIPMENT

spit roaster (see pp.232–33)
set of rotisserie spiked rods
charcoal fire
meat probe

THE PRACTICE

Shawarma Kebabs

Kebabs are the ultimate slow-cooked, handheld food – slices of spiced, wood-fired meat, sweet and juicy, wrapped in a grilled flatbread and served with a charred salad and cooling yogurt. As a young man, I had a weakness for a kebab after a late night on the town, but cooking this Middle East-inspired lamb recipe has redefined them for me and rekindled that once-guilty pleasure.

Figure a.

Figure b.

Figure c.

Method

01 Start by preparing your lamb shoulder. Cut the meat into large, thin slices less than 1cm (½in) thick. You are aiming to carve the meat into sheets with a good surface area, which you can then layer onto your spit, so the larger and thinner the better.

02 Once you have sliced the lamb, add the marinade. Sprinkle all the dry ingredients over the meat, then drizzle with the olive oil **(fig. a)** and massage into the lamb slices until they are evenly coated. Next, season the slices well with salt and pepper and add another drizzle of olive oil.

03 Place a set of square rotisserie spiked rods onto one end of the spit, and secure into place in the middle section for balance when cooking.

04 Feed your lamb slices onto the spiked rods, one at a time, to form the first layers **(fig. b)**; you want the herbs from the marinade sandwiched between the layers. Alternate the direction and placement of the slices on the spikes, from one piece to the next, so that all the lamb is tightly squeezed together in one mass. Repeat until all the lamb is layered onto the spit.

05 Feed another set of rotisserie spikes onto the other end of the spit and squeeze the two sets together to form one continuous kebab, held firmly in place.

06 Light a charcoal or wood fire 45 minutes ahead of cooking and when the embers are glowing, place your spit approximately 30–50cm (12–20in) above the hot coals. Cook the lamb for 2 hours 30 minutes, until the internal temperature is above 75°C (165°F) and the meat is juicy, rotating the spit by a quarter-turn every 15 minutes or so. Leave to rest for 30 minutes.

07 Once rested, carve the self-basted juicy kebab straight from the spit **(fig. c)**. Slice the Little Gem lettuces lengthways into quarters and char on a grill over the coals for 2–3 minutes, then slice thinly. To serve, fill the flatbreads with a generous serving of the warm lamb, the charred Little Gem, and a drizzle of yogurt.

EXPERT TIPS

Try using a motorised rotisserie attachment to rotate your kebabs. These can work really well and be set to run continuously at varying speeds, so you don't need to manually rotate the spit.

To avoid wasting any flavour, place a drip pan under the kebab to catch any juices and to avoid flare-ups when the fat hits the fire below. Use these juices to baste the kebab.

THE POSSIBILITIES

Keep It Turning

I love playing with marinades on a spit – baste whole poultry with herby butter, brush rolled or stuffed joints, or sandwich aromatics between layers of juicy meat.

ROTISSERIE REVOLUTION

Experiment with meats and flavours on a spit roast for hours of outdoor cooking fun.

- Goat meat is one of the most sustainable proteins you can source and the sweet flavour works well with Moroccan-style spices such as ras el hanout, pink peppercorns, dried rose petals, cumin seeds, and fresh mint **(fig. a)**.
- Alternate slices of pork shoulder with rounds of sliced pineapple, then glaze in teriyaki sauce with ginger for a sweet, sticky rotisserie.
- Experiment with thin slices of large root vegetables, such as spiced celeriac, for a slow-roasted vegetarian kebab.

LEAN BUT JUICY

Spit rotisserie is a great way to cook leaner meats without drying them out, because the meat is basted in its own juices as it turns.

- Try soaking hay in cider, beer, or wine before wrapping it around a whole chicken and securing with twine for a fruity marinade and a protective layer that keeps the bird moist.
- Also try spit-roasting pheasant wrapped in hay and served with chestnuts, apples, or ash-roasted stone fruits.
- A lean meat like venison can be great as a rolled haunch, stuffed with spiced plums and chestnut stuffing.

Figure a.

Figure b.

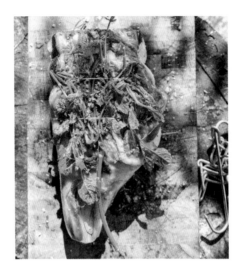

Figure c.

Figure d.

Try ... **Hay-roasted chicken** Stuff two 1.5kg (3lb 3oz) free-range chickens with 1 garlic bulb chopped in half, 1 orange cut into segments, and 4–6 sprigs of thyme, then season the skins with a generous pinch of salt and pepper. Next, soak a few large handfuls of meadow hay in a bucket of water (or cider, beer, or wine) for 5–10 minutes. Drain the hay, wrap it around the chickens in a 2.5cm (1in) layer, and tie in place with butcher's twine. Feed the birds onto a spit and roast for 1 hour 15 minutes until the juices run clear. Leave to rest and serve with grilled corn (**fig. b**).

GO SLOW

Whole joints can be asymmetrical and therefore harder to spit roast, but there are cheats.

- Hang a leg joint over a fire rather than spit roast. It can easily be rotated on a butcher's hook, lowered, or raised, for a slow, even roast.
- Lamb legs can be deboned and rolled with a layer of plants inside, such as nettles, wild thyme, and wild garlic, then cooked on a spit for a delicious foraged feast (**fig. c**).

Try ... **Lamb leg with roasted garlic and mint** Make 20 incisions 2cm (¾in) deep around the lamb leg, then push half a garlic clove into each hole. Tie on 12 sprigs of mint with butcher's twine and rub the lamb skin with 2 tablespoons of rosemary and horseradish salt mixed with 1 tablespoon of olive oil. Suspend the leg over a wood fire and cook for 5–6 hours until juicy and tender (**fig. d**), rotating it every hour and hanging it from the opposite end halfway through.

> "
> *The ingredients you add to a loaded spit roast are like veins of precious metals buried in ore. The gold is found when you carve into the layers and it's a delight to behold.*
> "

Project 25
WOOD-FIRED OVEN

Stone-baked delights with bubbling toppings and golden crusts.

SKILL LEVEL Medium:
working up the core
temperature of a fire for long
enough to heat a wood-fired
oven takes practice.

TIMINGS 1 hour or longer
for heating; 1–2 minutes
cooking at peak temperature.

Heat radiation
A wood-fired oven is a
winning combination of
physics and engineering.

THE SCIENCE

Thermodynamics

The thermodynamic principles at play in a wood-fired oven are never more prominent than in the dough crust and topping of a wood-fired pizza. The thermal conduction from the stone oven bakes the base, while the topping is cooked by thermal radiation reflecting off the domed roof and hot convection currents. Cooking from all angles using this triple heat source creates the ultimate balanced finish – and the magic of a wood-fired pizza.

THERMAL MASS

Wood-fired ovens have certain thermodynamic properties that conventional domestic electric or gas ovens can't match. Thermal mass is the ability to absorb, store, and then release energy as heat. Stone, clay, and brick – which are used to build a wood-fired oven – have a great thermal mass, which keeps the heat inside the oven more consistent. Strong absorbers of heat such as these materials are also strong emitters of heat. So as heat is generated, the internal mass of the thick oven walls and the floor absorbs the energy from that heat and then radiates it over an even cooking area. Radiant heat is transferred into the thermal mass of the oven by electromagnetic energy, typically via infrared radiation.

CONDUCTION, CONVECTION, AND RADIATION

The fire can be left in the oven while cooking, or it can be pulled out entirely, since the residual heat held in the structure itself is sufficient for cooking. The ideal temperature range is 350–425°C (660–800°F); at this point the internal temperature can remain constant for long enough to cook several pizzas evenly. The brick or stone floor has very good thermal conductivity, while the vaulted ceiling ensures that rising thermal rays bounce off the domed walls at different angles, creating super-hot convection currents that flow evenly around the space. It is this cycle of thermal conduction, convection, and radiation from above and below that provides the crispy crust of a pizza as well as the perfectly cooked toppings.

Heat transfer
There are three modes of heat transfer at work in a wood-fired oven – convection, radiation, and conduction – which together ensure an even bake.

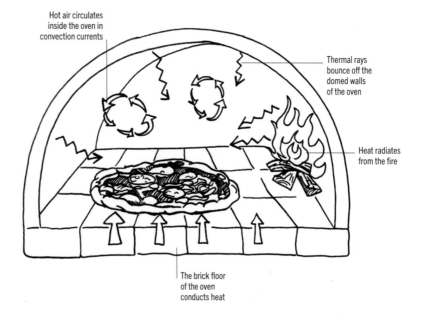

Hot air circulates inside the oven in convection currents

Thermal rays bounce off the domed walls of the oven

Heat radiates from the fire

The brick floor of the oven conducts heat

THE PRACTICE

Sourdough Pizza

This is my favourite rustic pizza. It doesn't need the usual tomato sauce but is still rich and creamy with melted mozzarella, herbs, and mushrooms. You need to stay focussed to prevent the dough from burning in the intense heat of a wood-fired oven, but the joy of sliding a pizza off a peel and into a volcanic oven, only to fetch it out and serve it still bubbling moments later, is unbeatable.

MAKES

4 pizzas

INGREDIENTS

For the bases
500g (1lb 2oz) organic strong
    white bread flour
150g (5½oz) sourdough starter
    (see pp.124–25)
250g (9oz) warm water
1 tbsp olive oil
1 tsp sea salt
For the topping
200g (7oz) mozzarella
200g (7oz) wild mushrooms
100g (3½oz) new potatoes,
    finely sliced
1 tsp olive oil
1 tbsp green olives, sliced
4–5 sprigs of rosemary, chopped
bunch of basil, chopped
sea salt and cracked black pepper

EQUIPMENT

dough scraper
banneton (proving basket)
wood-fired oven (ready made or
    see pp.244–47) or ceramic
    baking stone (see Expert
    Tips, right)
pizza peel
infrared thermometer

Method

01 First, make the dough for the bases. Mix the flour, sourdough starter, warm water, olive oil, and salt in a bowl with a dough scraper until a dough forms. Turn out onto a floured surface and knead for 10–15 minutes until the dough is smooth and springy, then form into a ball by folding the edges into the middle.

02 Place the dough ball seam-side down in a floured banneton, cover, and prove at 20–25°C (68–77°F) for 6–8 hours or overnight, until doubled in size.

03 Once proved, knock back the dough and divide into 4 equal-sized balls. Cover and leave on a tray to prove again for 1–2 hours at 20–25°C (68–77°F). The dough will rise just slightly. While you wait, light a wood-fired oven about 30 minutes before cooking (see p.247).

04 Once proved again, shape the dough balls into flat rounds by throwing them in the air **(fig. a)**. If you aren't confident trying this technique, stretch and flatten with your fists or fingers, or use a rolling pin.

05 Place the rounds on a floured peel, 1 or 2 at a time, and top with torn mozzarella, then mushrooms and sliced potatoes **(fig. b)**, both seasoned with salt and pepper and tossed in olive oil. Finally, garnish with the olives and chopped herbs. Check the oven temperature with an infrared thermometer, and once it has reached 330°C (625°F), place the pizzas in the oven using the peel and cook for 1–2 minutes until the mozzarella is melted and bubbling and the dough is puffed and crisp **(fig. c)**.

EXPERT TIPS

Pizza connoisseurs should aim for 330°C (625°F) as the optimum zone for a crispy base and cooked toppings. Get yourself an infrared thermometer and measure the oven-floor temperature rather than the internal space. This is because the emissive efficiency of a brick floor is nearly 100 per cent, making it ideal for accurate readings.

———

You can try to replicate the principles of a pizza oven in a domestic oven using a ceramic baking stone, which has similar physical properties to fire bricks in a wood-fired oven. If using, preheat the baking stone in the oven to 220°C (425°F) for 20–30 minutes before baking.

———

Pizzas with vegetable toppings that contain lots of water need more time in the oven, so add 1–2 minutes to the timer. Some pizza-makers lift the pizza base off the bottom with a wooden peel for 30 seconds before baking on the base of the oven to prevent the crust from burning while allowing the toppings to cook.

Figure a.

Figure b.

Figure c.

THE POSSIBILITIES

Ultimate Al Fresco

With a hot oven at your disposal, you can experiment with all sorts of dishes and use the intense heat to roast in trays, bake on the oven floor, or cook dishes in pans.

CHARRED VEGETABLES

A wood-fired oven can transform vegetables dramatically with little effort, as the sugars char into the sweetest umami textures.

- I've reinvented baba ganoush by baking a whole aubergine for 10–15 minutes in a wood-fired oven until soft in the middle and encased in a fragile smoky skin. Stuff with feta, chilli, and mint, then top with a raw egg yolk, yogurt, and tahini dressing **(fig. a)**.
- Salt-baking whole vegetables such as pumpkin or beetroot **(fig. b)** is a great way of protecting them from the intense heat of a wood-fired oven. It also seasons them evenly and adds a sea-mineral tang.

- Bake whole corn on the cob for 10–15 minutes and, once cooked, strip back the husks and finish on the oven floor to char the kernels. Strip the corn and blitz with hummus and harissa. Serve with popped corn, 'nduja (see p.182), and olive oil for a colourful starter **(fig. c)**.

Try ... Salt-baked vegetables Mix 500g (1lb 2oz) plain flour, 200g (7oz) sea salt, and 4 beaten egg whites in a bowl and wrap the mixture around the vegetables. You can add herbs or hay to the salt dough for added flavour. Bake in a wood-fired oven at 330°C (625°F) for 10–15 minutes until the veg are tender. Serve with wilted kale, berries, and yogurt.

Figure a.

Figure b.

Figure c.

Figure d.

Figure e.

WOOD-FIRED STEAK

You can cook a steak in a pan, on a grill, or dirty on a bed of charcoal, but if you want the real deal, try a wood-fired steak.

- Surf 'n' turf can be a luxurious combination to try in a rustic wood oven. Lobster with seaweed butter, flat iron steak, and some hispi cabbage is stunning **(fig. d)**. To serve, wrap the delicate lobster claw meat in a blanched cabbage leaf, secure with a cocktail stick, brush with a little tarragon oil, and bake for 1 minute.
- Not all steaks are meat. Rub a whole cauliflower with coconut oil, turmeric, and cumin seeds before roasting whole. It will only need 3–4 minutes, then carve into steaks and garnish with yogurt, flaked almonds, mint leaves, and pomegranate seeds **(fig. e)**.

SPICE UP YOUR ROASTS

Roasted meats take on big flavours in a wood oven and they cook amazingly quickly.

- Silverside beef coated in a spiced dry rub and then cooked with spiced butter is a great twist on a normal roast. Serve with pink pickled onions, cauliflower florets, Bombay potato salad, and wilted spinach.

Try ... Spiced silverside beef Make a dry rub with 1 teaspoon of coriander seeds, 1 teaspoon of black onion seeds, 1 teaspoon of garam masala, and 1 teaspoon of chilli flakes. Place 500g (1lb 2oz) beef silverside in a skillet pan and rub with the spices. Next, coat the beef with 2 crushed garlic cloves mixed with 2 tablespoons of olive oil. Transfer to a hot oven and bake at 330°C (625°F) for 5 minutes, then remove and add 50g (1¾oz) salted butter to the pan. As it melts, spoon the butter over the beef, then return to the oven. Cook for another 10 minutes, then leave to rest for 10 minutes before serving.

> *This type of cooking brings people together more than most. The fire builds, excitement builds, we feast together in the heat, then there's a slower communion as the warmth starts to die.*

THE PRACTICE

Make a Clay Oven

Treading the cob to build a wood-fired oven with local materials is a job that goes backs hundreds of years where I live in Cornwall. It involves physically stamping and squashing the straw, sand gravel, clay, and water together by foot – you could use a cement mixer, but where's the fun in that? It's heavy work, but great fun, and overall it's an intuitive, forgiving project for a first-timer.

Figure a.

Figure b.

Figure c.

MAKES

1 large clay oven

INGREDIENTS

50kg (8 stone) cement mortar
2 sq m (21½ sq ft) heat-storage
  bricks
2 tonnes (315 stone) sharp sand
47 x 47 x 5–10cm (1½ft x 1½ft x
  2–4in) piece of solid oak with a
  handle, cut into an arched shape
1,000 litres (220 gallons) water
1 tonne (160 stone) clay
1 straw bale
2m (6½ft) chicken wire
50kg (8 stone) lime render

EQUIPMENT

shovel
mallet
spirit level
wire brush
tarpaulin
tape measure
newspaper
bucket
shears
wire cutters

Method

01 Start by building the base of your oven. This needs to be located on firm foundations to support the weight of the structure. Spread the cement mortar over an area of 2 square metres, then lay the bricks in a square on the surface, with a doorstep of 1 brick's width at the front. Try to keep the bricks flush together and use a mallet to gently tap them into the mortar as you lay them. Use a spirit level to try to keep the base flat **(fig. a)**. As a finishing touch, you can also add a wooden trim around the brick base if you wish.

02 Gently brush the surface with a wire brush, then cover with tarpaulin and leave for 24–48 hours until the mortar has set.

03 Next, use about one-third of the sand to build a large dome in the centre of your base **(fig. b)**. Build the dome so that it is 1m (3½ft) across and 60–75 per cent of the diameter in height – so 75cm (2½ft) tall. Position the piece of oak at the front of the dome – this will be the oven door. The door must be 63 per cent of the inner dome height, so, for these proportions, it should be 47cm (1½ft) tall. If the height of your dome is different, multiply the height of your sand dome by 0.63 to calculate your door height.

04 Once you have built a uniform sand dome, spray gently with water from a hose or watering can to dampen the surface. Then place a layer of newspaper all over the surface **(fig. c)**. Repeat with 2–3 more layers.

continued >

Figure d.

Figure e.

Figure f.

05 Next, using half the clay and another third of the sand, make a mixture of 1 part clay to 2 parts sand. An easy way to do this is to place a few buckets of the sand and clay in the middle of a large tarpaulin and dampen it with 1 bucket of water. With a friend, take a corner each and pull the tarp across to one side so that the mixture folds over itself. Then pull back the other way to fold the mixture again. Repeat but in the opposite direction, changing the angle by 90°.

06 Next, test the consistency of the clay and sand mixture to see if it is moist enough. You should be able to form a ball that holds together enough to juggle with it **(fig. d)**, rather than crumbling apart. It should feel soft and easy to squeeze in your fingers. If it is too hard, add more water and repeat the mixing process.

07 Now build the first layer by forming the clay into brick-sized pieces and pressing them against the base of the dome **(fig. e)**. Compress into place and work your way around the whole dome, building around the door and maintaining an even 8cm (3in) thickness, until you reach the top. Once you've covered the whole dome, smooth the surface slightly **(fig. f)**.

08 Next, make the cob by mixing the remaining clay and sand as before, using the same 1:2 ratio, and adding

water as needed to reach the same consistency. To incorporate the straw, cut it into smaller pieces first with shears, then sprinkle it over the surface of the clay mixture. Now start mixing it in with your feet. Keep treading the cob until the straw, sand, clay, and water are all thoroughly mixed together **(fig. g)**. You should be able to squash the cob into balls and shape it between your hands without it falling apart.

09 Start building up a layer of cob that's at least 15cm (6in) thick around the dome **(fig. h)**, until you reach the top. Press the handfuls of cob into each other and maintain the thickness all the way round.

10 Now cover the dome with tarpaulin to protect it from rain and leave to dry for 2–3 weeks. After the first week, remove the door and carefully scoop out the sand dome by hand, so that the oven can dry inside and out.

11 The final stage is to render the external surface of the dome once it has completely dried out and the surface is no longer tacky to touch. If you cover the cob dome with a layer of chicken wire, this will help the render stick and support the integrity of the structure. I recommend a lime render made of lime, cement, clay, and sand in a ratio of 1:1:1:3. This will take a couple of days to dry.

Figure g.

Figure h.

12 Before you cook with your oven, you must cure it. Start by building a very small fire on day 1 with just a handful of kindling. Make a slightly larger fire each day and after 3 or 4 days you should be able to light a full-blown fire inside.

13 When ready to cook with your oven for the first time, build a small fire inside with kindling and, once it takes, add a couple of logs at a time. Try to build a fire that develops an intense hot core, then wait for 30 minutes to allow the embers to burn down. Once the embers turn to white ash, remove them from the oven with a shovel or slide them to one side.

14 Measure the temperature of the oven floor with an infrared thermometer. It should be 300–450°C (570–840°F) for cooking; 330°C (625°F) is the optimum temperature for cooking most things.

15 To cook, place your food inside the oven and seal the opening with the door. I always soak the door in water for an hour or so before cooking so that it doesn't burn or warp.

EXPERT TIPS

Another test to ascertain if the cob is ready to build with is to roll a clay sausage and hold half of it in your palm, letting the other half dangle over your hand. If the clay bends but doesn't break, it's ready to use.

⸻

If the walls of your oven are too thin or the cob walls haven't dried out before your first firing, cracks can appear in the walls. If these do occur, you can use a high-heat silicone to seal them or apply additional wire mesh and add another layer of clay and render.

⸻

It is very easy to repair a clay oven. Damage to the external layer is common, so try to keep spare supplies of the cob and render ingredients for patching.

INDEX

THE ARTISANS

ANDY APPLETON

Chef

Andy is a self-taught chef, learning most of his skills from the many amazing chefs he has worked with in his career, and developing his passion for food by travelling the world (particularly Italy). Most recently, Andy spent nine years as the head chef of Jamie Oliver's Fifteen Cornwall, and before that he was at the award-winning flagship restaurant Fifteen London, overseeing the apprentice chef training programme that has graduated 101 young chefs into the industry. Andy left Fifteen in February 2016 to start Appleton's at the Vineyard. Today, he runs Appleton's Bar & Restaurant in Fowey, Cornwall.

www.appletonsrestaurant.com

FRANCIS CLARKE

Dairy

Francis Clarke is the managing director of Trewithen Dairy, an award-winning dairy company based in the heart of Cornwall. The Clarke family began processing milk and cream and delivering it to local shops more than 20 years ago. Today, with a highly skilled team of over 200 staff, the Trewithen family produce delicious milk, cream, butter, and yogurt using milk from herds within 25 miles of their family farm in the beautiful Glynn Valley. Trewithen Dairy is a true Cornish success story.

www.trewithendairy.co.uk

MARC DENNIS

Charcuterie

Marc is the sole owner and producer at Duchy Charcuterie. He has a passion for food and for meat in particular. He has built up his award-winning cured products business from scratch and takes great delight in creating new and exciting flavour combinations, pushing the boundaries of British charcuterie. When he is not in the production room, he can be found at the BBQ smoker or in the kitchen, incorporating some of his own products into delicious dishes for his family, such as the very popular 'nduja pasty and Christmas favourite, smoked turkey wrapped in home-cured pancetta.

www.duchycharcuterie.co.uk

TOM HAZZLEDINE

Sourdough

Tom Hazzledine was just 23 when he tried his hand at baking bread for his local farm shop. Before long, he was supplying handcrafted bread to many local shops, markets, cafés, and restaurants, and now runs five bakeries and an ever-expanding wholesale business in the Southwest of England. "The key to a great sourdough", Tom says, "is using your own wild starter. Mine was created years ago and has been nurtured and used in all our loaves ever since. It helps create the complex, wholesome flavour, addictive tang, and satisfying crust that every good sourdough needs."

TY MCKEND

Smoking

Ty and his family are passionate about all things smoky: live-fire grilling, *asado*, fire roasting, low 'n' slow American BBQ, curing, and cold smoking. Cooking with fire has always brought them together. Ty's father started ProQ Barbecues & Smokers back in 2008, and since then they've been producing the best-quality BBQ smokers, smoking woods, accessories, and cold-smoking equipment available, providing everything you need to take your love of food to the next level.

www.proqsmokers.com

GIEL SPIERINGS

Cheese

The Cornish Gouda Company was founded in 2012 by Giel Spierings when his family dairy farm was no longer viable. At 17, Giel went back to his home nation of the Netherlands, where he learnt the skill of artisan Gouda. He brought the knowledge back to Cornwall, where he converted an old outbuilding at his parents' dairy farm. The business has gone from strength to strength and is now producing multi-award-winning cheese. Cornish Gouda is produced using sustainable forestry and a biomass boiler together with solar panels to make the business more sustainable.

www.cornishgouda.co.uk

BARRIE GIBSON

Cider

Barrie is the master cidermaker at Fowey Valley Cider in Cornwall. He makes a very special multi-award-winning champagne-style cider and an easy-drinking bottled session cider called Castledore. He also distils his cider to make an eau de vie, a pommeau, and a wonderful oak-aged cider brandy. He runs occasional courses and tastings, which can be booked on the Fowey Valley website, where you can also buy all of his products.

———————

www.foweyvalleycider.co.uk

ROSE GREENE

Fermentation

Rose is a chef and the co-founder of 4Hands Food Studio, in the midlands of Ireland. Fermentation has been part of her life for many years now, after immersing herself in the wild and wonderful ways of ancient preservation techniques while working alongside the microbiology department of Antwerp University. With her partner, Margaux Dejardin, she produces naturally fermented drinks and vegetables at 4Hands Food Studio. Together, they preserve and capture the flavour and nutrition of each month to develop an extensive larder for use in Rose's dining experiences.

———————

Instagram @4hands_food_studio

EDWARD HART

Outdoor Cooking

Edward Hart is a massive lover of all things outdoors and enjoys nothing more than cooking and eating outside with his family. He lives on the moor near St Neot in Cornwall and his connection to that landscape is something that defines him. He is always looking for excuses to bring people together at his pop-up restaurant Narrada to share outdoor cooked food, with a bit of music and a great menu from James thrown into the mix.

BARBARA TAMBLYN

Butter

Barbara has lived at Botelet Farm in Cornwall since 1956, when she married her husband David and moved to his family's farm. Most of Barbara's life has been spent taking care of the people and spaces at Botelet. She has always loved creating, whether in the kitchen, in the garden or crafting, and her pasties are second to none – a skill still to be learnt by the next generation!

TIA TAMBLYN

Plant-based Food and Preserves

Tia's love of plant-based cooking, simple gatherings, and wellbeing are fused together in Botelet Breakfast Club – the monthly pop-up café that Tia hosts along with her husband Richard at the family farm in Cornwall. Tia also works as a massage therapist, offering treatments and running workshops at Botelet. When not in the kitchen or therapy room, she can normally be found wild swimming in quiet coves or walking the coastal path with Richard and their three young children.

———————

www.tiatamblyn.com
www.botelet.com/breakfast

PHILIP TANSWELL

Salt

Philip Tanswell is the managing director of the Cornish Sea Salt Company and a self-confessed salt geek. When not peering through microscopes at minerals, Philip loves nothing more than spending time at his shoreline house, cooking for his family in their outside kitchen over wood. Cracking the alchemy of pretty tasty sea salt flakes has led Philip to look further into the science and benefits of the various salts that are found in the oceans and their application to health and wellbeing. "Proper unrefined sea salt is brilliant," he says. "Not only is it essential for life, it also tastes good as well. Salts are as different as wine."

———————

www.cornishseasalt.co.uk

ACKNOWLEDGEMENTS

ABOUT THE AUTHOR

James Strawbridge is a Cornish chef, sustainable living expert, and presenter. James is passionate about reducing food waste and encouraging people to spend more time outdoors cooking, foraging, and gardening. He presented the TV cooking shows and environmental programmes *The Hungry Sailors*, *It's Not Easy Being Green*, and *Saturday Farm*, and has made recent cooking appearances on *Escape to the Chateau*. James co-founded the Sons of Thunder agency to offer marketing consultancy, art direction, food photography, recipes, and product development to artisan food and drink brands. In his spare time, he helps to home educate his three young children with his wife, Holly.

AUTHOR'S ACKNOWLEDGEMENTS

I'd like to thank my wife, Holly, for her support and patience while I've been writing this book. It's taken a long time to produce; working from home on the writing, illustrating, and shoots is hard enough, but sharing a small space with our home-educating family means we've had to work as a team. You've been amazing and I couldn't have done it without you. And thanks so much for all the beautiful pottery that makes this book look and feel authentically artisan. I can't wait to shoot another with more of your wonderful ceramics – please, make me more plates!

Next, I'd like to thank John Hersey, the photographer for *The Artisan Kitchen*, co-founder of www.sonsofthunderagency.com, and my good friend. Working with you on this book has been so much fun. From day one, whether shooting on the moor, on the beach for a Cornish clambake, or in the home studio, you brought such positive vibes and incredible skills. Thank you for your hard work, trust, professionalism, and friendship.

Julian from The Soho Agency is the most excellent agent to work with and it's been an absolute privilege. He has removed any feelings of anxiety or stress, and been a calm and supportive influence. I really hope we can work together again in the future on more books.

Mary-Clare has been a feature of the DK team for a long time but also in my life for over a decade. Thank you so much, MC, for your support, and I wish you all the best in retirement – I look forward to taking you to lunch in Cornwall sometime. A big thank-you to everyone who has worked on this book, especially Alastair, Holly, Karen, Miranda, and Saffron, also Dawn, Maxine, Lucy, Luca, and Tony. You've all been amazing to work with and you make publishing what it is: polite, professional, and lovely – it's certainly my favourite industry to be a part of, because of how you all are to work with!

Finally, thank you to all the guest artisans who came along to help out for a day and share their time, ideas, energy, and expertise. Lifestyle gurus Tia and Richard at Botelet, fire legend Ed, butter aficionado Barbara, fermenting goddess Rose, chef Andy, milk man Francis, curing maestro Marc, master cidermaker Barrie, baker Tom, smoking renegade Ty, cheese legend Giel, and salt geek Philip.

PUBLISHER'S ACKNOWLEDGEMENTS

Dorling Kindersley would like to thank Steve Crozier for retouching, Marie Lorimer for indexing, and Anne Newman for proofreading.